P9-DNF-375

ALS—
LOU GEHRIG'S
DISEASE

Other titles in Diseases and People

AIDS
0-7660-1182-8

ALLERGIES
0-7660-1048-1

ANOREXIA AND BULIMIA
0-7660-1047-3

ARTHRITIS
0-7660-1314-6

ASTHMA
0-89490-712-3

CANCER
0-7660-1181-X

CARPAL TUNNEL SYNDROME AND OTHER REPETITIVE STRAIN INJURIES
0-7660-1184-4

CHICKENPOX AND SHINGLES
0-89490-715-8

COMMON COLD AND FLU
0-89490-463-9

DEPRESSION
0-89490-713-1

DIABETES
0-89490-464-7

EPILEPSY
0-7660-1049-X

FOOD POISONING AND FOODBORNE DISEASES
0-7660-1183-6

HEART DISEASE
0-7660-1051-1

HEPATITIS
0-89490-467-1

LEUKEMIA
0-7660-1310-3

LYME DISEASE
0-7660-1052-X

MEASLES AND RUBELLA
0-89490-714-X

MENINGITIS
0-7660-1187-9

MONONUCLEOSIS
0-89490-466-3

MULTIPLE SCLEROSIS
0-7660-1185-2

RABIES
0-89490-465-5

SEXUALLY TRANSMITTED DISEASES
0-7660-1050-3

SICKLE CELL ANEMIA
0-89490-711-5

TUBERCULOSIS
0-89490-462-0

—Diseases and People—

ALS— LOU GEHRIG'S DISEASE

Mary Dodson Wade

Enslow Publishers, Inc.

40 Industrial Road   PO Box 38
Box 398   Aldershot
Berkeley Heights, NJ 07922   Hants GU12 6BP
USA   UK

http://www.enslow.com

Library of Congress Cataloging-in-Publication Data

Wade, Mary Dodson.
    ALS—Lou Gehrig's disease / by Mary Dodson Wade.
        p. cm. — (Diseases and people)
    Includes bibliographical references and index.
    ISBN 0-7660-1594-7
    1. Amyotrophic lateral sclerosis—Juvenile literature. [1. Amyotrophic lateral sclerosis.
    2. Diseases] I. Title: Lou Gehrig's disease. II. Title. III. Series.
    RC406.A24 W33   2001
    616.8' 3—dc2l   00-009429

Printed in the United States of America

10 9 8 7 6 5 4 3 2 1

To Our Readers:
We have done our best to make sure all Internet addresses in this book were active and
appropriate when we went to press. However, the author and the publisher have no control
over and assume no liability for the material available on those Internet sites or on other Web
sites they may link to. Any comments or suggestions can be sent by e-mail to
comments@enslow.com or to the address on the back cover.

Illustration Credits: Colin Bell, p. 83; Corel, p. 19; Courtesy of the National
Library of Medicine, pp. 23, 27; Díamar Interactive Corp., p. 62; Dover
Publications, Inc., p. 11; Enslow Publishers, Inc., p. 55; Harold Wade, pp. 32, 35,
37, 38, 40, 41, 46, 47; Intel, p. 99; Linda Gibson, p. 44; PhotoDisk, p. 72; Sunrise
Medical, pp. 86, 87, 88; World Book Encyclopedia, p. 93.

Cover Illustration: Dover Publications, Inc.; Intel; Linda Gibson.

Contents

Acknowledgments

ALS is a devastating disease. It leaves patients, families, doctors, and friends helpless to alter its course. Hope is on the horizon, but it is not here yet.

In writing this book, I wished to honor my friend, Harold Lott, for whom the cure did not come soon enough. I also want to acknowledge my admiration for his wife, Bobbye, and other caregivers like Linda Gibson, who shared their stories with me.

Several Web sites, such as the ALS Association, were helpful. I particularly appreciate the clarity and range of the information found on the Ride for Life Web site and on ALS patient Steve Shackel's Web site. I applaud their efforts to put a face on this terrible disease.

ALS—LOU GEHRIG'S DISEASE

WHAT IS ALS? A disease that causes muscles to cease to work. About half of ALS patients live for two to five years after diagnosis.

WHO GETS IT? The disease can strike anyone. At least 10 percent of ALS cases are inherited.

WHAT ARE THE CAUSES? Little is known about the cause. The inherited form is related to a gene on chromosome 21.

WHAT OCCURS WHEN ALS DEVELOPS? Neurons that carry messages from the brain to the muscles shrivel and die. Without them, muscles cease to move. As a result, the patient becomes paralyzed.

WHAT ARE EARLY SYMPTOMS? Patients may stumble or feel clumsy. Muscles twitch and cramp. Speech becomes slurred. In final stages of the disease, patients can hear and see but cannot move.

HOW IS ALS IDENTIFIED? No one test can say positively that a patient has ALS. No one test can rule out the disease. Doctors run many tests involving the muscles and the brain. They look for loss of both upper (brain to spinal cord) and lower (spinal cord to muscle) motor neurons.

HOW CAN IT BE PREVENTED? No one knows.

HOW IS ALS TREATED? Since the cause is not identified, there is no cure. One drug, riluzole, slows down the disease slightly. Treatment consists of helping patients cope with their worsening condition.

WHAT IS THE STATUS OF RESEARCH? Researchers are seeking both cause and cure for ALS. They are encouraged by recent developments, but as yet nothing stops the disease or reverses the effects.

1

Lou Gehrig: Great Man, Terrible Disease

The stands grew hushed. Sixty-two thousand people trained their eyes on the tall figure standing in the middle of the New York Yankees' baseball diamond. Everybody there knew him. They had come to honor Henry Louis Gehrig.

Gehrig was there to say goodbye. Yankee Stadium had been his home during his fourteen years in the major leagues. This was the only team he ever played for.

His prowess at bat had helped the Yankees win six World Series Championships. They would win again that year, but his hitting would not be bringing in runs.

As he stood in the middle of the field that July 4, 1939, Gehrig praised everyone else. He paid tribute to the fans. He praised fellow players. He spoke about his family's support.

He refused to be beaten down. "Fans," he said, "for the past two weeks you have been reading about the bad break I got. Yet today I consider myself the luckiest man on the face of this earth."[1]

Lucky? No one else there considered him lucky. Lou Gehrig was dying of amyotrophic lateral sclerosis (ALS). Few people even knew what the disease was. But they admired Gehrig's courage and saluted his remarkable career.

Terrific Player

Lou Gehrig was born in New York City in 1903. He was the son of working-class parents. He knew the sacrifices they had made to help his career. And he had learned from them the value of working hard. That willingness to work helped him develop his baseball talents.

After finishing high school, the strapping young athlete enrolled at Columbia University. His six-foot frame carried 200 pounds. He played both football and baseball.

It was his ability to hit the baseball, however, that caught the eye of a New York Yankees' scout. The Yankees signed him to a contract.

He spent the next three years with their minor league farm team in Hartford, Connecticut. Then, in 1925, he won a berth as first baseman on the great Yankee team.

Gehrig was a formidable hitter. His lifetime average was .340. The batting order placed him behind legendary Babe Ruth, but his powerful talent still earned him honors.

Baseball great Lou Gehrig suffered from ALS.

In 1927, when Ruth hit 60 home runs, Gehrig matched him for most of the season. He fell behind when Ruth's bat suddenly went wild. Gehrig ended the year with forty-seven home runs. Taken together, these two Yankee players produced more home runs in 1927 than the entire team output for every other franchise in the league except one.

Twice, in 1927 and in 1936, Gehrig was chosen Most Valuable Player. In 1934, he won the Triple Crown. This honor is based on having top scores in batting, home runs, and runs batted in. In a career that spanned 1923–1939, Gehrig collected a total of 493 home runs. Twenty-three of them were grand slams. He was the first player to hit four home runs in a single game.

Gehrig's reputation, however, did not rest solely on his ability to hit. He played in 2,130 consecutive games. That record earned him his nickname, "The Iron Horse."[2]

His record for the most consecutive games played stood for fifty-six years. It was broken on September 6, 1995, when Baltimore Oriole Cal Ripkin, Jr. stepped onto the field to play.

Signs of Trouble

In 1936, Gehrig led the American League in home runs and runs scored. That was the year the Yankees began a run of four straight World Series championships.

By the time the 1939 contest came, however, Gehrig was no longer in the Yankees' lineup. The previous year, his batting average had nose-dived. He lost the strength to hit long balls. Home runs eluded him. He was hitting flies and making outs.

Then, a friend noticed that Gehrig shuffled his feet as he walked. The baseball star went to several doctors who puzzled over his symptoms. One treated him for gall bladder problems. His condition continued to worsen.

During the last game he played, Gehrig had trouble getting back to first base to catch a ball that would put the batter out. His teammates spoke of his "good play." To him, this level of performance was unacceptable.

Gehrig was responsible for making up the batting roster before each game. The next day, the manager was startled to see that Gehrig's name was missing from the lineup. The great player had taken himself out of the game.

Not long after that, Lou Gehrig learned that he had amyotrophic lateral sclerosis (ALS). He would never play again. Two years later, ALS claimed his life.

Honoring a Legend

The people who filled Yankee Stadium that day in 1939 knew that they were looking at a legend. Not only was Gehrig an outstanding athlete, but he was also respected for his personal qualities. He had a reputation for being kind, courteous, and thoughtful.

Because of the high regard for him as a player, the Baseball Hall of Fame inducted him early. Rules for admission required that a player be retired for five years before becoming eligible. Gehrig was installed just six months after he left the game.

ALS—No Respecter of Persons[3]

People in all walks of life get ALS:

- Hall of Fame pitcher Jim "Catfish" Hunter died of ALS in 1999.

- That same year, ALS claimed editor Ruth Whitney. During her thirty-one-year career at *Glamour*, she shaped the magazine into a thought-provoking forum for women's issues.

- Boxing champion Ezzard Charles had ALS.

- Football player and coach Bob Waters contracted the disease.

- Vice-president Henry Wallace, who served during Franklin Roosevelt's third term, had the disease.

- New York Senator Jacob Javits suffered from ALS.

- Composer Dimitri Shostakovich had ALS.

- Movie actor David Niven was stricken with ALS. When he became unable to speak his lines clearly, mimic Rich Little dubbed them in.

- Michael Zaslow earned an Emmy for daytime television drama. In his last role, Zaslow played the part of a man dying of ALS. His own death from ALS came a year later.

The Yankees organization honored him as well. They retired his uniform. Nobody else will ever wear his number.

In Monument Park, located just beyond center field fence, the Yankees honor their great players and managers. Gehrig's number 4, surrounded by traditional Yankee pinstripes, is there, along with memorials to other Yankee greats.

Lou Gehrig's Disease

Lou Gehrig died June 2, 1941. He was thirty-eight years old when ALS took his life.

The scientific name of the disease is almost unpronounceable. It is much easier to remember the name of the famous baseball player whose career it cut short. Many people simply call it Lou Gehrig's Disease.

2

ALS—History of a Puzzle

ALS causes muscles to stop working. The disease is not contagious, but it is fatal. In only 2 percent of the cases do doctors know any reason for the disease to occur. And, although doctors are hopeful, at the present time there is no cure.

The scientific name, *amyotrophic lateral sclerosis*, is easier to understand when broken into parts. The first word holds the key. It has three scientific word parts:

A = not having any

myo = muscle

trophic = food or nourishment

Literally, this means "no food for the muscle." When that happens, the muscle will not work.

The reference is to the loss of lower motor neurons. Lower motor neurons run from the spinal cord to the muscle. They carry messages that stimulate the muscles. This activity keeps the muscles healthy—it is their "food." When a patient has ALS, the messages stop, and the muscle dies.

The second word, *lateral*, really means "to the side." The neurons that carry messages to muscles enter and exit from the side of the spinal column.

Sclerosis, the third word, means "scarred" or "hardened." Taken together, these last two words describe what happens to upper motor neurons, the ones that runs from the brain to the spinal column.[1]

Both upper and lower motor neurons are necessary for muscles to contract and make the body move. In ALS, a breakdown occurs. Neurons are not able to pass the message from the brain to the muscle. Without the impulse or message, muscles stop moving. After a while, they become rigid and waste away.

The brain is where muscle contraction starts. Upper motor neurons bring the message down through the spinal cord. In the spinal cord, the message is picked up by the lower motor neurons and sent on to the muscles. ALS disrupts the flow of messages to the muscles. It took many centuries for people to understand the connection between the brain, the spinal cord, and the muscles.

In Ancient Egypt

Five thousand years ago, ancient Egyptians learned about bodies as they prepared mummies. But they did not see the connection between the brain and the spinal cord.

Egyptians had no regard for the brain. To them, the heart was the center of the being. As they prepared bodies for burial, the embalmers put the heart and other organs such as the liver in beautiful jars. These jars were placed in the tomb near the mummy.

Egyptians regarded the brain as being part of the skull. The skull is bony. Bones have marrow. To them, the brain was simply the soft, fatty tissue that fills the cavities of most bones.

Embalmers took the brain out through the nose. This method of removal hid the fact that the spinal cord links the brain to the rest of the body. They simply threw away the most important organ in the body.[2]

Hieroglyphs on the Brian

In spite of this, Egyptians did understand that head injuries were dangerous. The first recorded use of the word *brain* is found in an ancient papyrus called the Edwin Smith Surgical Papyrus.[3]

Edwin Smith, an American Egyptologist who was born in 1822 and died in 1906, bought the papyrus while traveling in Egypt in 1862. The papyrus, a medical document that contains information dating from five thousand years ago, is in the form of a doctor's journal. It may have been a medical textbook. In it, the doctor describes his patients' injuries, then states how he will treat the problem.

The first twenty-seven cases are skull injuries. Six others deal with injuries to the neck.

Case #6 contains the first mention of the brain. The doctor notes that the patient's skull has been "smashed." Through the gaping hole, he can see the soft, wrinkled, throbbing mass inside the skull.

The doctor knew he could not help this victim. He came to the same conclusion that he did with most of the other head injuries. It was "an ailment not to be treated."

Case #31 deals with someone who seems to have fallen head-first. The doctor describes neck vertebrae that telescope in upon each other. In addition to many other symptoms, the patient could not hold his head up. The

The first recorded use of the word "brain" is found in an ancient Egyptian papyrus.

19

doctor does not mention seeing anything that could have been the spinal cord.

Greeks Celebrate the Brain

Two thousand years later, the Greeks built a culture that prized the human body. Around 440 B.C., a Greek doctor named Alcmaeon of Croton wrote a book about the body. While dissecting animals, he observed connections running between the eyes and the brain. He announced that the brain controlled everything.[4]

Another famous Greek doctor, Hippocrates, rightly surmised that the brain was involved in thought and sensation.[5]

Before long, a controversy was raging. Two of Greece's greatest thinkers, Plato and Aristotle, took opposite views on which organ controlled the body. Plato agreed with Hippocrates. He said that the brain was in charge of actions and thought. Aristotle, on the other hand, argued that the heart was the center of our being.[6]

Romans on the Right Road

During Roman times, a doctor known as Rufus of Ephesus put together a book called *On the Names of the Parts of the Human Body*. This book, published sometime around 100 A.D., showed that the brain and the nerves were connected.[7]

Then, Galen of Pergamum, another Greek doctor, began to study the body. He wrote many books. In 177 A.D., he gave a lecture entitled "On the Brain."

Galen performed surgery on live monkeys. He described what happened when he cut the spinal cord. "After the incision, in all the nerves which lie below the place where the transection has been made, both the two potentialities are lost, I mean the capacity of sensation and the capacity of movement."[8] The animals could neither feel nor move below the place where he cut the spinal cord. He saw clearly that the spinal cord carried the messages to the muscles.

Because of his work with the spinal cord, Galen opposed Aristotle's views about the heart. This controversy between the supremacy of the brain or the heart lasted until the end of the Middle Ages in the 15th century.

Light After the Dark Ages

For thirteen centuries following Galen, very little new information about the nervous system came to light. Then, in 1543, Andreas Vesalius, a Flemish doctor, published his book, *On the Workings of the Human Body.*

Heartfelt Emotions

Remnants of Aristotle's idea that the heart controls emotions remain today. A heart shape is used in written messages as a substitute for the word *love.* Valentine's Day cards read, "I love you with all my heart."

For the first time, a medical book showed accurate pictures. Until that time, medical artists could only guess how the interior parts of the body looked. Religious doctrine did not allow autopsies.

In his book, Vesalius included horizontal "slices" of the human brain. He gave the first indication that different regions of the brain control different functions of the body. He correctly showed nerves running from the brain to all areas of the body.[9]

Little by little, scientists uncovered the secrets of the nervous system. In 1717, Dutch scientist Antoni van Leeuwenhoek used his newly-invented microscope to examine nerve cells. He noted that each nerve cell had a long projection sticking out like a root. This is called the fiber.

Leeuwenhoek did not know the significance of the fiber. Another hundred years would pass before German neurologist Robert Remak would give the name *axon* to the cell fiber.[10] (A neurologist is a doctor who makes a special study of the nervous system of the body.) By the time Remak named the fiber, it had become clear that messages travel through the axon and pass to the next cell.

The manner in which muscles are stimulated became clear when Italian scientist Luigi Galvani noticed that frog legs in his laboratory were twitching. The frog legs had picked up electricity while lying on a metal plate during a thunderstorm. In 1791, Galvani published a paper describing how tiny amounts of electricity make muscles move.[11]

In the early 1800s, Remak spent a great deal of time dissecting rabbits. He observed that some nerve cell fibers had a white coating around them. He called this covering *myelin.*[12]

Myelin-covered fibers are the ones that carry messages, but scientists did not yet know how the message system worked. German scientist Otto Friedrich Karl Deiters turned his attention to the tiny projections that sprout from a nerve cell body. These projections are called *dendrites.*

By 1865, Deiters had learned that axons pass the message to the dendrites on the next cell.[13]

In 1717, Dutch scientist Antoni van Leeuwenhoek used his newly-invented microscope to examine nerve cells.

Bushy Dendrites

In 1889, Wilhelm His, a German anatomist who taught at Basel and Leipzig, came up with the name *dendrites* for the projections sticking out of a nerve cell body.[14] The projections look like little bushes. The word "dendrite" means *trees*.

Fitting the Pieces Together

At the end of the nineteenth century, there was a wealth of information about the nervous system, but it was scattered among different research publications. Wilhelm von Waldeyer, a German anatomy professor, brought it together.

Waldeyer was a prolific writer, but none of it was based on his own research. He simply drew information from many sources and compiled it in an organized manner. He published this information in a series of scientific journal articles.

To make his explanations easier to understand, Waldeyer included drawings. Some were his own. Many were based on the work of other scientists. The illustrations presented accurate pictures of neurons running from the brain to the spinal cord and from the spinal cord to the muscles.

Waldeyer borrowed heavily from Spanish scientist Santiago Ramon y Cajal. In 1889, Ramon y Cajal startled the scientific community when he announced that neurons do not touch. A tiny space exists between them, and the message jumps across.[15]

Ramon y Cajal's work was honored in 1906 when he and Camillo Golgi received the Nobel Prize for their studies of the structure of the Nervous System.[16]

Several years after Ramon y Cajal's announcement about neurons, English scientist Charles Scott Sherrington gave the name *synapse* to the space between nerve cells.[17]

When the System Goes Haywire

As doctors learned more about how the different parts of the nervous system worked, they began to understand why it sometimes breaks down. The breakthrough for ALS occurred in 1850 when Augustus Waller, an English scientist, described the appearance of shriveled nerve fibers.[18]

Fibers are normally full and healthy. Shriveled fibers are not able to transmit messages. Waller's description of shriveled fibers provided the key that would eventually unlock the puzzle of how ALS affects the body.

Naming Neurons

Wilhelm von Waldeyer added a number of words to the scientific vocabulary that deals with the nervous system. He gave the name *neuron* to the combination of a nerve cell body and the fiber extending from it.[19]

Jean-Martin Charcot

The man who identified and gave ALS its name was a French doctor named Jean-Martin Charcot.[20] Born in Paris in 1825, Charcot was the son of a carriage maker. He was a brilliant student and entered the University of Paris medical school at age nineteen.

After graduation, he spent most of his career at the Salpêtrière. This large hospital outside Paris provided humane care for patients with mental and physical problems. It became Charcot's laboratory. There, he observed poor, aged patients who suffered from many types of chronic illnesses.

He followed patients over the long course of their diseases. After a patient died, the doctor performed an autopsy to find out what had physically happened. The autopsies showed clearly how a particular disease affected different organs of the body.

Knowledge gained from those autopsies explained the observations he had made in the patient's condition. Charcot understood what was happening internally. He became an expert in diagnosing a patient's problem while it was in the early stages.

Charcot concentrated on patients with neurological problems. He developed an extraordinary ability to identify closely related diseases. He was the first to identify multiple sclerosis. Charcot recognized it in a man who worked for him before the man knew anything was wrong.

Beginning in the early 1870s, Charcot wrote important papers on diseases. Among them were classic descriptions of ALS and multiple sclerosis.

His description of ALS appeared in Lecture XIII at the Salpêtrière in 1878. The lecture was entitled "On Amyotrophic Lateral Sclerosis." Three years later, it appeared in English in a three-volume edition of *Lectures on the Diseases of the Nervous System.*

Jean-Martin Charcot (center) was the man who identified ALS and gave the disease its name. France recognized Charcot's work by calling the disease his name.[21] In Great Britain, the disease is called Motor Neurone Disease, or MND. MND uses the British spelling of the word *neuron.* ALS is a term used worldwide.

The medical school at the University of Paris rewarded Charcot by appointing him professor of nervous system diseases. This was the first recognition of neurology as a specialty in medicine.

Although Charcot was not an easy person to get to know, he was an extraordinary teacher. Students from around the world flocked to his classes. They sat spellbound while Charcot used real patients to demonstrate how a disease affects the patient.

The distinguished physician and lecturer died in 1893. His explanation of ALS was so accurate that it remained valid long after his book passed its hundredth birthday.

Sigmund Freud

One of Charcot's students was physician Sigmund Freud. Freud's ideas about a mental condition called *hysteria* were ridiculed at the time he stated them. Patients diagnosed with hysteria appeared to be blind or paralyzed. But doctors could find no apparent reason for their problems. Ridicule of Freud continued until Charcot declared that hysteria was a real disease.

However, this illness puzzled Charcot. In every other disease, he had been able to find an underlying physical cause for a patient's symptoms. Charcot could find no physical condition as the basis for hysteria.[22]

There is almost no mention of ALS before Charcot gave his description. Perhaps the disease did not occur before the middle of the nineteenth century when he described it.

Perhaps it is only coincidence that the disease became known at a time of dramatic change in the way people lived. The century between 1760 and 1850 is called the Industrial Revolution. During this time, machines took over many jobs that had previously been done by hand. It is interesting to note that ALS made its appearance at the time that the Industrial Revolution occurred.[23]

3

Movement—
Brain to Muscle

Harold Lott was a successful contractor and real estate developer in Houston, Texas. Among other things in his busy life, Lott maintained an active role in his church. Along with his wife, Bobbye, he served on boards of charitable organizations.

In his mid-fifties, Lott jogged five miles a day to stay in shape. Then he began to stumble. He changed to bike riding but had a bad wreck. At that point, he turned to an exercise machine.

He had difficulty walking. He assumed that this was related to surgery for a ruptured disk in his back. Finally, though, he consulted a neurologist.

The doctor listened to a story of stumbling and strange muscle cramps. Then the doctor observed a sign that Lott himself had not noticed—a quivering tongue.

The doctor suspected ALS and ordered a battery of tests to rule out other causes. The tests supported his diagnosis.

Although Lott was a private person, he talked openly about his disease. He continued to work, using an electric scooter to get around.

On the last day of his life, Lott drove his van to his office. He returned home that night, exhausted but looking forward to the dedication of the lodge at Trinity Pines the following week. The religious encampment was special to him. Even as his strength waned, he had continued work toward the completion of the project.

One week after Lott's funeral, Trinity Pines held the dedication ceremony. His wife and two children were there as the worship center on the second floor was dedicated in his honor.[1]

The Brain as Master Control

ALS destroys muscles by interrupting the system of messages that keeps them working. These impulses originate in the brain.

This organ is about the size of a grapefruit. It weighs about three pounds and has the consistency of a raw egg. It is the body's master control room.[2]

The Cerebrum

When people speak of the brain, they are generally referring to the cerebrum. The cerebrum takes up more space in the skull than any other part of the brain.

31

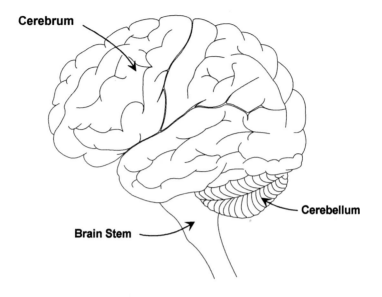

Cerebrum

Cerebellum

Brain Stem

The brain has three major areas, but it is the cerebrum and the brain stem that are affected by ALS.

The cerebrum is highly developed in human beings. It directs the ability to see, hear, smell, taste, and feel sensations. It is the center of learning. It governs the ability to think, to use language, and to feel emotions.

The cerebrum has two layers. The extremely thin outer layer is called the *cortex*.[3] The cortex is the information processing part of the brain. Sometimes it is jokingly referred to as our "gray matter." It is a creamy gray color because of the nerve cell bodies found there.

Underneath the cortex, a mass of whitish-colored neurons fill the rest of the cerebrum. This part is called white matter.

Billions of fibers sprout from the cell bodies. The white color comes from the glistening myelin coating around the fibers.

The cerebrum's surface is creased and wrinkled. A deep valley runs down the middle of the brain from front to back.

Other Parts of the Brain

Although the cerebrum occupies most of a person's skull, other areas have important functions. The area called the *cerebellum* is much smaller than the cerebrum. In fact, the cerebellum is sometimes called "the little brain."

The cerebellum lies beneath and behind the cerebrum. Its purpose is to coordinate movements. It helps with balance and keeps movements from being jerky.

A third part of the brain, the *brainstem,* is the downward extension that leads to the spinal cord. The brainstem controls involuntary movements such as breathing. These are actions that we never think about and do not consciously control.

The brainstem is so smoothly connected to the spinal cord that it is impossible to tell where one ends and the other begins. The spinal cord descends from the skull through vertebrae to an area just below the ribs.

Grooves in the Brain

A crease or groove on the surface of the brain is called a *sulcus.* The high place between grooves is called a *gyrus.*

33

Neurons are Message Carriers

There are about 100 billion neurons in the brain.[4] Messages flow to and from the brain along a highway that consists of two different kinds of neurons. Each has a distinctive shape.

One type is called sensory. They pick up sensations. Two thread-like fibers run in opposite directions from a bulging "head" (cell body). Sensory neurons form a two-way corridor that carries messages to and from the brain.

The other type is a motor neuron. These neurons allow us to move. The enlarged "head" of the motor neuron is the cell body with its nucleus, or center. Springing out in all directions from the cell are dendrites. Also emerging from the cell is a single long fiber. The fiber leads either to the dendrites of the next cell or to the muscle.

Messages travel down the axon, or cell fiber. The end of the axon branches out. When the message reaches the end of these multiple endings, the message jumps across the synapse to dendrites located on other cells.

The message is carried across the synapse by a chemical agent called a *neurotransmitter*. Glutamate is a neurotransmitter for motor neurons.

Long Fibers

Some motor neurons have fibers that are quite long. The longest one in the body is about three feet. It runs from the spinal cord to the heel.[5]

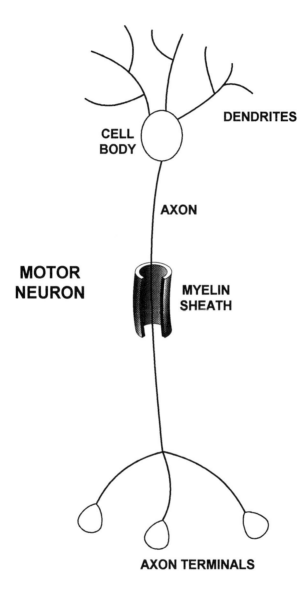

The myelin-covered fiber, called an axon, carries messages from the dendrites on this cell body of the motor neuron down to the terminals, where the message is relayed to the next motor neuron.

Message Movers

Neuro refers to neurons. *Trans* means "across" and *mitter* refers to "send." A neurotransmitter sends the message across the synapse from one neuron to the next.

Glutamate delivers the impulse from the axon to "ports," or receptors, on the dendrites of the next neuron. The receptors accept only those neurotransmitters that are exact matches.[6]

When the message enters the dendrites of the next neuron, something like a tiny explosion occurs. This energy propels the message on its way down the axon. This continues until the message reaches the muscle.

Motion Starts in the Motor Cortex

The cerebrum has roughly four physical divisions. Each of the right and left halves of the brain has another thin but deep crosswise groove, or sulcus, about midway back.

Scientists have known for a long time that different sections of the brain control different actions and abilities. Motor neuron messages originate in the motor cortex of the brain. This part is located just in front of the deep crosswise groove. It runs across the cerebrum much like a hairband. The area is called the precentral gyrus. *Precentral* loosely means "in front of the middle."

Tiny electrical impulses, or messages, leave the motor cortex and descend to the muscles. Unlike sensory neurons,

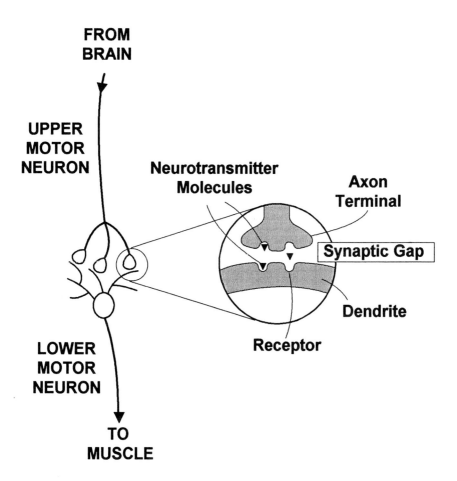

Messages travel from the brain to the muscle. Neurotransmitters carry the message across the synapse to the dendrites of the next motor neuron.

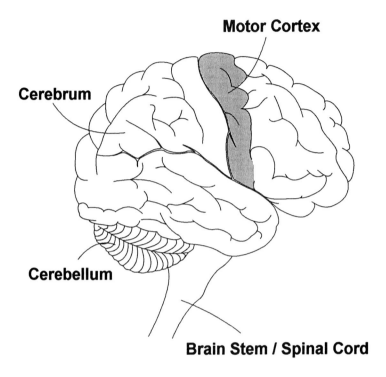

Motor Cortex

Cerebrum

Cerebellum

Brain Stem / Spinal Cord

Messages that move muscles begin in the motor cortex of the cerebrum.

motor neuron messages travel in one direction only—from the brain to the muscle.[7]

The neuron messages work together like this: Suppose you open the door when you return home. Sensory neurons in your nose send a message to your brain. The brain remembers this smell. The brain sends messages to the muscles in legs and feet so that you walk to the kitchen.

Sensory neurons in the eyes report to your brain that a plate on the counter contains circular objects with small, dark lumps in them. Sensory neurons in your nose also bombard your brain. "Ah," says your brain, "chocolate chip cookies!"

At this point, the brain sends a message down the motor neurons to your fingers. "Pick up a cookie," it says. It tells muscles to open your mouth. Next it tells your hand to put the cookie in your mouth. Then it tells your jaw muscles to chew. The brain does not need to tell your throat to swallow. Those muscles work without your thinking about it.

Sensory nerves on your tongue confirm that eating the cookie was a good thing. The brain sends a message to your hand to reach for another cookie, and the same thing happens again. You do not want to stop.

Relaying Messages on Motor Neurons

It takes two sets of motor neurons to move muscles—upper motor neurons and lower motor neurons. The spinal cord is the switching station between them.

Upper motor neurons run from the brain to the spinal cord. The spinal cord has a center core that is shaped like a butterfly. Areas that stick out to form the "wings" are called *horns.*

Anterior (front) horns are located on the front side of the spinal column. The anterior horn area is the place where the switching occurs. In this area, messages carried by the upper motor neurons pass to the lower motor neurons.

This action is much like passing a baton between relay runners. After lower motor neurons receive the message, they exit the spinal column. They run from the spinal cord to the muscle. Once the message reaches its destination, the muscle moves.

39

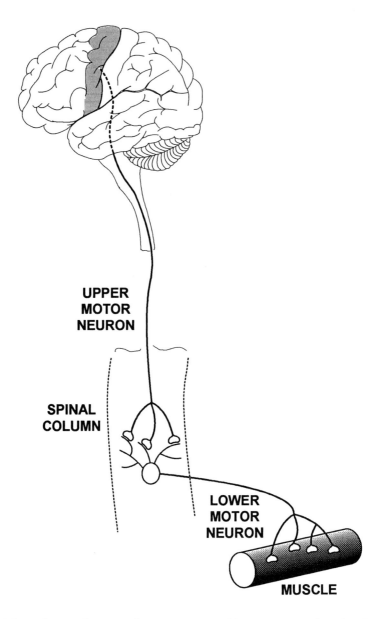

UPPER
MOTOR
NEURON

SPINAL
COLUMN

LOWER
MOTOR
NEURON

MUSCLE

The exchange of messages between upper and lower neurons takes place in the spinal column.

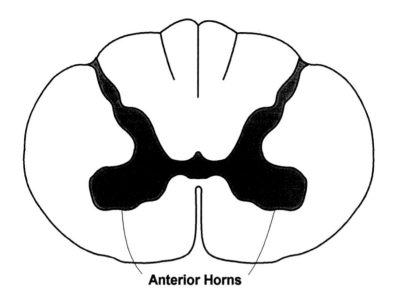

Anterior Horns

Anterior horns are located on the front side of the spinal column.

ALS Targets Highly Developed Nervous Systems

Humans have motor neuron connections that allow them to do incredibly complex jobs with their hands and fingers. In humans, a huge number of cortex neurons are used to make precision hand movements.[8]

Humans are able to perform complex actions that involve several groups of muscles. For example, when singing, people use muscles in the face, throat, chest, and diaphragm to produce the sounds. Sometimes while doing that, the performer may also be playing a musical instrument. ALS strikes this complicated interconnection of nerves.

Animals and ALS

Animals do not get ALS. For one thing, most animals do not have the complicated nervous system that ALS affects. Apes are the exception. However, apes do not get ALS for the same reason other animals do not—they just do not live long enough.[9]

ALS Mosaic

ALS does not affect all areas of the brain. Motor neurons in both the cerebrum and the brainstem are involved, but the disease does not affect the cerebellum.

Even though ALS targets motor neurons, it is selective about which ones it attacks. It does not affect the heart or the eyes. Patients retain bladder and bowel control.

Neither does ALS affect sensory neurons. Patients are still able to think, hear, see, smell, taste, and feel skin sensations.

As ALS destroys more motor neurons, patients lose first one set of muscles then another. In the short span of a few years, the patient, although alert, loses all voluntary movement. Unless the person has breathing assistance, death occurs when muscles that control breathing cease to work.[10]

4

What is ALS?

Marcie Gibson had been a competitive gymnast since she was nine years old. The Arlington, Texas, native began her cheerleading days in junior high school and continued them through college.

She chose Exercise and Sports Studies as her college major, with Dance as a minor. In addition, she taught gymnastics to earn money for expenses. But her greatest dream was to be a cheerleader for the Dallas Cowboys.

She knew that competition for a position on a professional cheerleading squad would be fierce. In 1993, with one semester to go in college, she took additional dancing lessons. One night, as she was doing a dance routine, she found that she could not keep her arms above her head. This puzzled her.

That summer, she concentrated on her acrobatic skills by attending a cheerleading camp. The workouts at the camp

At the age of twenty-three, Marcie Gibson learned that she had ALS.

involved tumbling and other gymnastic routines. The routines were challenging, but should not have been difficult for her. To her surprise, she fell on her head several times. For someone as experienced as Gibson was, this should not have happened.

The family became concerned and took her to see a doctor. Six months of testing followed. Then, just a few weeks before time for the Cowboys' cheerleader tryouts, Marcie Gibson learned the truth. At the age of twenty-three, she had ALS.[1]

ALS Destroys Neurons

The first thing most ALS patients notice is muscle weakness. This may be as simple as having trouble tying shoes or buttoning a shirt. Or it may be as disconcerting as being unable to keep your balance when walking. Sometimes the first symptoms occur as speech or swallowing problems.

The symptoms may be mild at first, and those having problems may not consider their situation to be serious. They assume there is a simple explanation. Perhaps an inner ear problem caused trouble with balance. Perhaps there is some chemical lacking in the body that could be corrected with vitamins or supplements.

Even if they have something as serious as a brain or spinal cord tumor, these are often treatable. Patients can make full recoveries. Not so with ALS. There is no cure.

Life expectancy for ALS patients averages two to five years. Half live at least three years. Twenty percent live five years or more, with up to 10 percent surviving more than ten years.[2]

ALS Survival Rate

10% live more than 10 years

10% live 5–10 years

30% live 3–5 years

50% live less than 3 years

Scientists do not know why a person gets ALS, but they do know the process that occurs. The symptoms the patient experiences are caused when muscles atrophy (waste away). Something has interrupted the flow of impulses from the brain to the muscle. Motor neurons are dying.

As the damaged neurons shrivel, they pull away from the muscle. The person to whom this is happening will not be aware that anything is wrong until the muscle weakness shows up. The shriveled neurons cause no pain in the process of detaching from the muscles.

A muscle has more than one neuron attached to it. At first, only part of them are affected by the disease. Movement continues as long as some of the neurons are working. ALS may have destroyed up to 80 percent of the neurons before muscle weakness and atrophy are evident.[3]

ALS occurs most often to persons between the ages of forty and seventy. The average age when the disease becomes apparent is about fifty-five years. But there are cases of patients much younger and of people who were in their eighties when they were first diagnosed.[4]

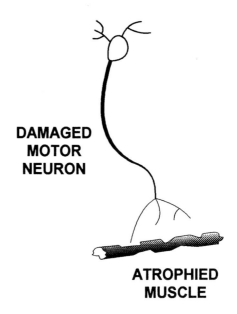

DAMAGED
MOTOR
NEURON

ATROPHIED
MUSCLE

As the damaged neurons shrivel, they pull away from the muscle.

47

ALS does not often strike young people. If young people get the disease, however, they usually live with the disease longer than older patients.

In some age groups, more men than women have ALS. When the disease begins at age fifty-five or earlier, one and half times more men than women will be diagnosed. However, from ages sixty and up, gender makes no difference. At that point equal numbers of men and women are reported among new cases of ALS.[5]

ALS is the most common of the degenerative diseases of the nervous system.[6] There are about 5,000 new cases in the United States each year. Because the death rate from ALS almost matches that of new cases, the number of ALS patients remains almost constant. Statistics from the United States National Institutes of Health indicate that there are approximately 30,000 Americans who have ALS at any given time.[7]

ALS occurs throughout the world. Currently, 350,000 people worldwide have the disease.[8] It attacks persons without regard to race, ethnic group, or economic status, but occurs more often in temperate zones.[9]

Where Does it Start?

Robin Balsdon, an electrical engineer, was born and educated in South Africa. He immigrated to Australia in 1980 and worked in the computer field. He enjoyed a variety of sports, especially those related to the ocean.

Balsdon's first indication of trouble was a tendency to stumble. Soon, he had to abandon his passion—surfing. At age forty, he no longer had strength to ride the waves. It took many doctor visits before he learned that he had ALS.[10]

Balsdon's case is fairly typical of the way patients become aware something is wrong. He first noticed a problem with his legs. When ALS begins in the arms or legs, it is called *limb onset.* This is the most common place for the disease to begin.

Sometimes, the first signs of the disease involve problems speaking or swallowing. This is called *bulbar onset.* Neurons that control the mouth, tongue, and jaw originate in the widened part of the brainstem called the medulla, or bulb. Bulbar refers to that area. Involuntary muscles governed by the brainstem control breathing and swallowing.

Doris Dillon's first indication of ALS was a slowing of her speech. The San Jose, California, teacher made her lively classroom a place where children enjoyed learning to read. As one colleague put it, she could "teach a rock to read."

In 1997, Dillon began to have speech problems. Her ALS had bulbar onset.

Voluntary Muscles Fail First

In the late nineteenth century, John Hughlings Jackson, British neurologist, studied progressive muscle diseases. He noted that voluntary muscles—the ones we consciously control—usually fail before the involuntary ones, over which we have no conscious control.[11]

Dillon refused to give up contact with the children. She took a position running the library. There, she could share stories, especially ones about people like Lou Gehrig. Volunteers acted as her voice.

Everyone knew that she had ALS. Mothers and teachers praised her openness. "They [students] have learned that if something like this happened to them, they wouldn't have to hide. They could go on."[12]

Regardless of which onset occurs, ALS is progressive. Once fibers begin to shrivel, there is no way to stop the process. People who first noticed a problem walking will eventually lose the ability to speak and breathe on their own. People who first noticed trouble swallowing will lose the ability to use their arms and legs.

Once patients become unable to eat or breathe, their only method of survival is a feeding tube and a ventilator to provide oxygen.

Sporadic ALS

ALS is classified into three different forms. The most common form is called *sporadic*. The name comes from the random or sporadic way it occurs. There is no identifiable reason why the disease attacks a particular person. Perhaps when scientists identify a cause for ALS, the disease will get another name. It may not be random at all.

Sporadic ALS is sometimes referred to as classical ALS. This is the form described by Charcot. It accounts for 90 percent of the cases.[13]

Familial ALS

Five to ten percent of ALS cases are an inherited form called *familial.*[14] In inherited diseases, a parent passes along a defective gene to the next generation. Sometimes the effects of this are easily recognized, but familial ALS is not that easy to identify. This form of the disease looks just like sporadic ALS. It causes the same kind of neuron damage.

Familial ALS is recognized only when the disease develops in more than one member of the immediate family. This includes grandparents, parents, siblings, uncles, and aunts.

Families with familial ALS are often not aware that they are targets of the disease. A man in Washington state did not give a second thought to the muscle aches he was experiencing. After all, he was still in his thirties.

Then he got a call from his brother in California. The brother described strange twitches and cramps in his legs. He could not grip things with his hands. Finally, after consulting many doctors, the California brother was calling family members to tell them that he had ALS.

Families With ALS

Doctors suspect that the percentage of familial cases may actually be higher than official figures indicate. Some sporadic cases could be familial.[15] Only after obtaining full family histories can a doctor know of other occurrences in the family.

To the brother in Washington, the words came as a double shock. He was deeply concerned for his brother. He also realized that the symptoms he was hearing about were the exact things that were happening to him.

As the two talked, they recalled their grandmother, who had died twenty years earlier. She had been a lively character who had taken the boys on trips before she had been forced to stop driving. She had often talked about her "mysterious and rare disease." The brothers realized that she must have been suffering from ALS, the disease that was attacking them. Three cases in one family—the disease had to be inherited.[16]

When a family has been identified as having familial ALS, the children have a 50 percent chance of being affected.[17] In the case of the West Coast brothers, they developed the disease, but their two sisters did not.

Familial ALS follows some genetic laws but not others. Some inherited diseases skip a generation. Sometimes only the sons are affected and the daughters transmit the defective gene. This is not true with ALS.

In familial ALS, the disease passes from one generation to the next without skipping. Both men and women can be affected. Both genders can pass the gene along. The two brothers traced their disease to their grandmother, who had passed the disease to their father, who then passed it to them.

We receive our traits from our parents through the genes they pass on to us. The genes are found in chromosomes. A human being has cells that contain 46 chromosomes. One half of the chromosomes come from one parent, and one half from the other parent.

Chromosomes are threadlike structures that contain long strands of DNA. Genes are arranged in order along the strand. The structure of a person's DNA is what makes that person unlike anyone else.

Sometimes, something changes the normal arrangement of genes on the strand. When this happens, the gene does not produce the right effect. In 1993, scientists identified a defect on chromosome 21. This chromosome contains a gene that normally produces an enzyme called superoxide dismutase (SOD1). Researchers now know that a mutant SOD1 gene is associated with ALS.

The percent of familial patients with this defective gene is very small. Only 2 percent of all cases of ALS are related to it.[18]

There are tests to show whether a person has the defective gene, but some people do not want to know. They do not wish to worry. To them, it is better to deal with the problem if and when it occurs.

But there is hope even if a person has the defective gene. Not everyone with the mutation develops ALS.

For identical twins, however, there is no question. If one twin develops the disease, the other will also get it. In one case, it took eleven years after the first twin was diagnosed for the second twin to have recognizable symptoms.[19]

ALS has no set timetable to occur. It is possible for a child to develop familial ALS before the parent does. This occurs because of the great variation in the age of onset. In the case of the two West Coast brothers, their father began to have symptoms a year and a half after they were diagnosed.

Guamanian ALS

A third form, *Guamanian,* is confined to small areas in the Pacific.[20] The main place is the island of Guam in the western Pacific Ocean. That gives this form its name. The number in this group is very small.

Guamanian ALS became known in the 1950s when an epidemic occurred among the Chamorro people on the island of Guam. There were 50 to 100 times more cases of ALS there than in populations elsewhere. Oddly enough, between 1960-1985, the occurrence rate among the Chamorros leveled out to match the rest of the world.[21] Patients with Guamanian ALS experience the same loss of motor neurons as do sporadic patients. However, the Chamorro group has some unique features. Three times as many men are affected as women. Also, patients have longer survival times. They live about twelve and

Familial ALS Strikes Earlier

The age at which patients with familial ALS are diagnosed is usually ten years younger than those with the sporadic form. The disease may develop more rapidly in these patients. First signs usually occur in the legs.[22]

Guamanian ALS became known in the 1950s when an epidemic occurred among the Chamorro people on the island of Guam, but cases of Guamanian ALS are not confined to Guam. High concentrations of the disease have been found in the Mariana Islands and western New Guinea. Many cases occurred in the Kii Peninsula on the Japanese island of Honshu. Regardless of where this form of ALS occurs, however, it is usually referred to as Guamanian.[23]

a half years after diagnosis, as compared to two to five years for most ALS patients.[24]

Because Guamanian ALS is concentrated in certain areas of the Pacific, researchers thought that there must be some local connection. They hoped to find clues to reveal what caused ALS.

They ruled out close contact between the Guamanian groups because they do not live near each other. Neither do the people have any common cultural or genetic factors.

Some people thought that the Guamanian form was familial ALS. But Guamanian ALS does not follow regular hereditary laws. In addition, there are no cases involving the defective gene on chromosome 21.[25]

Nearly forty years ago, nutritionist Marjorie Whiting blamed the Chamorro diet for the large number of ALS cases. The Chamorros ate a tortilla-like bread made from the flour of ground-up nuts of the cycad (false sago) plant.

Cycad nuts are poisonous. Knowing that, the Chamorro people soaked them in water for several days to remove the toxin. After three days, they gave the water to their chickens. If the chickens got sick, the nuts went back for extra soaking.

Scientists found that cycad nuts contain an unusual amino acid. This, however, did not provide a link with other ALS cases. If the amino acid in the nuts caused Guamanian ALS, then the same amino acid should be found in sporadic patients as well. It is not there.[26]

Other researchers thought that mineral imbalance might be causing Guamanian ALS. They knew that rats that eat foods low in calcium and magnesium develop ALS-like symptoms. Also, high levels of aluminum and iron, plus the lack of calcium and magnesium, cause neurons to die. However, the researchers were unable to prove that mineral imbalance contributed to Guamanian ALS.[27]

Even though each of the three forms of ALS has some slight variation specific to it, all ALS cases are clinically the same. The disease destroys motor neurons. What follows is relentless muscle failure.[28]

As fibers of the motor neuron shrivel, the affected neurons die. At first, messages are intermittent because only part of the impulses connect with the next neuron. Gradually, though, upper motor neurons pull away from their terminal points in the spinal column. This causes anterior horn cells to die.

ALS and Dementia

Guamanian ALS has one symptom that is not found in other forms. In some cases, patients may have ALS, dementia, and Parkinson's disease all at the same time. The dementia is the result of tangled nerve fibers such as those that cause Alzheimer's disease. The occurrence of all three diseases in one patient is puzzling. Neither ALS nor Parkinson's patients normally suffer mental impairment.[29]

Without the message from the upper motor neuron, the lower motor neurons cannot function. Shriveled fibers of lower motor neurons pull away from the muscles.

Eventually, all messages stop. Without stimulation, the muscles waste away. Amyotrophic lateral sclerosis has done its work. The ALS patient, fully aware of everything that is going on, lies trapped in a body that will not move.

5

Diagnosing ALS

During the last ten years, the number of ALS cases has risen. This may be due to the fact that people are living longer. Some doctors consider aging neurons to be a trigger that causes a person to get ALS.[1]

One reason may be that better medicine has allowed people to survive diseases that would have killed them fifty years ago. Another factor is that doctors have better tools to use in diagnosing ALS. But diagnosis is still a long process.

There is no one test that will prove that a patient has ALS. And there is no single test to rule it out. Doctors must eliminate other diseases as the cause of the patient's problem. Until they do this, they cannot confirm a diagnosis of ALS.

Much of the difficulty lies in the symptoms. Doctors are trained to recognize illnesses by signs they observe in patients. But this very thing complicates the diagnosis. Because ALS shares so many symptoms with other diseases, the doctor may not suspect the real cause.

Correct diagnosis is important both for the ALS patient and those who do not have ALS. Many of the diseases with symptoms similar to ALS are treatable. It is important to start treatment for patients who have a chance of recovery.

Signs the Doctor Observes

One of the symptoms of ALS is twitching muscles. ALS patients experience rapid twitches called *fasciculations.*[2]

Healthy persons also have fasciculations, but the ones that ALS patients experience are likely to be in unusual places. The doctor may examine the patient's tongue. The easiest place to observe fasciculations in an ALS patient is the tongue.[3] The patient may not even be aware that this is happening.

The most common symptom of ALS is painful muscle cramps. Of course, healthy people get leg cramps too. Runners drink lots of water because dehydration causes muscle cramps. However, ALS patients suffer cramps in their hands, jaw, abdomen, neck, or tongue.[4]

Fascicle—a Muscle Cable

Nerve fibers come in bundles. These bundles look like a cable with many strands. This "cable" is called a *fascicle.* Fasciculations occur when the fascicle twitches.

In spite of the fact that no pain is associated with the shriveling of the nerve fibers causing the disease, ALS patients experience intense pain. This comes from muscle cramps and from joints where muscles are out of balance because of atrophy.

Doctors check for *spasticity* or rigidity. Spasticity occurs when both sets of muscles remain tense—both the one in tension and the one that should be relaxed. Not everyone with spasticity has ALS, but everyone with ALS will eventually develop spasticity.[5]

Another sign doctors look for in ALS patients is hyperreflexia. Hyperreflexia is an overreaction of the muscle when a tendon is tapped.

You have probably dangled your legs over the side of the examination table at the doctor's office. When the doctor tapped just below the kneecap with a small "hammer," your foot kicked out. This is a normal reflex action caused by the tendon in the knee being struck.

It would seem logical that muscles damaged by ALS would be too stiff to respond. On the contrary, ALS patients exhibit too much reflex. That is true unless the muscle is totally paralyzed.

Another procedure that doctors can perform is a check of the extensor plantar reflex. The test involves moving a not-too-sharp instrument along the side of the foot.

A normal reaction during a check of the extensor plantar reflex would be for the toes to curl under. If the patient has brain damage, however, the toes will spread and the big toe

Muscles at Work

Muscles work in pairs. One muscle relaxes while the other is in tension. When you raise your hand to your face, your elbow bends. This allows the biceps to relax. At the same time, your triceps lengthens and tightens. You have put tension on the triceps.

When you straighten your arm, the opposite happens. The triceps relaxes. The biceps is now in tension. An athlete doing "curls" at the gym gives both of these muscles a workout.[6]

will point upward. The same thing occurs with the loss of motor neurons such as occurs in ALS. This test for brain or spinal cord damage is so simple that it can be used with babies as young as a year and half.[7]

Doctors also check patients for symmetry. Our body is built with two sides that are almost mirror images—two arms, two legs, two lungs. Even the head has matching sides.

Diseases and syndromes such as strokes, brain tumors, and polio will affect one side of the body but not the other. That is not the case with ALS. Muscle weakness may begin on one side of the body. But, over time, the matching muscle on the opposite side of the body will be affected as well.[8]

Tests Done in the Laboratory

The most common testing done when any person goes to the doctor's office is based on blood and urine samples. ALS patients have these same tests done in order to rule out other diseases.

Urine is collected over a twenty-four hour period and tested for heavy metals such as lead or mercury, and even aluminum. High levels of some metals in the body cause damage

Hyperreflexia

Hyper means "over" or "too much." *Reflexia* refers to "reflex action" or a movement that you do not consciously control.[9]

Babinski Reflex

Extensor plantar reflex is sometimes called the Babinski Reflex. Joseph Babinski, a French doctor, first described this reaction in 1896.[10]

to tissue. Lead intoxication can cause ALS-like symptoms of muscle weakness and twitching, as well as increased reflexes.[11]

ALS-like symptoms occur when thyroid or parathyroid hormones are not at the correct level. If the blood tests show that thyroid hormone levels are normal, then the doctor can rule out hyperthyroidism as the cause of the patient's problem. But that does not necessarily mean that the patient has ALS.[12]

Doctors look at levels of parathyroid hormone. ALS patients have normal levels of this hormone. If test results are high, there may be a tumor on the parathyroid. Surgery can correct that.[13]

When upper motor neurons are affected, the doctor will order a spinal tap. ALS patients usually have normal or only slightly elevated levels of proteins in the spinal fluid. If the levels are high, something other than ALS is the problem.[14]

A muscle biopsy is done to obtain a small sample of tissue. This is examined for any change in muscle fiber shapes.[15]

A cross-section of a normal muscle fiber shows densely packed areas that look something like the end of a fistful of angular dry spaghetti. Shriveled muscle fibers, on the other hand, have irregular shapes and sizes. This indicates muscle atrophy.

Wasted muscle tissue is one of the results of ALS, but other diseases can cause the same effect. Doctors must conduct more tests before they form a diagnosis.

Machines that Test Electrical Impulses

Several different machines are available to test the ability of neurons to conduct electrical impulses. These tests indicate abnormal nerve and muscle activity in the early stages.

Electromyography (EMG) measures the muscle's electrical impulse. The test requires that a needle be inserted in the muscle, an uncomfortable procedure. During the test, a continuous line of jiggles with spikes appears on the screen. When ALS neuron loss is severe, the spikes will be quite pronounced.[16]

An EMG can confirm the loss of anterior horn cells early in the disease. It also detects loss of muscle strength. It will confirm that breathing muscles are affected even before this is evident.

Biopsy

In a biopsy, the surgeon removes a tiny piece of tissue. By examining the tissue under a microscope, the doctor can see whether the tissue is healthy or has something wrong with it.

Another test is called Nerve Conduction Velocity (NCV). It measures the time needed for an electrical impulse to travel down a known length of nerve. In ALS, the rate at which the electrical impulse moves is normal. If the electrical signal is slower or weak, some other disease is at work.[17]

Pictures of the Body

Doctors have long used X-rays to look at broken bones. However, X-rays are of little value in diagnosing ALS. Doctors need to look at soft tissue to rule out ALS as a cause of the patient's problems.

Magnetic resonance imaging (MRI) is a procedure that uses a strong magnet to line up atoms inside the body. The person is surrounded by a powerful magnet. Radio waves bombard the nuclei of the atoms in the body. The atoms of different types of tissue display distinct features on the computer screen.[18]

MRI images allow doctors to spot problems such as hardened tissue in the brain. Hardened brain tissue occurs with multiple sclerosis, but not ALS.

MRIs can reveal the presence of spinal diseases and tumors. These conditions can cause weakness, twitching in the arms, atrophy, and stiffness in the legs, but they are not ALS-related.

Computerized Tomography (CT), formerly called a CAT scan, uses X-rays to make pictures of the brain. The word *tomography* comes from the Greek word that means "slice." X-rays are beamed from six hundred different angles through the skull to a sensor located on the opposite side of the head. A screen displays pictures of all the different angles of the brain. If the images reveal a tumor or blood clot in the brain, that will explain the patient's problem and rule out ALS.[19]

Positron Emission Tomography (PET) presents color images of brain activity. Tiny amounts of radioactive dye are injected into the brain. When a person does something as simple as raising an arm, the screen lights up with different colors in the area of the brain that is working.

PET images will show dark areas in the brains of patients who have Alzheimer's or have suffered a stroke. These are the damaged areas where no activity is taking place. ALS does not affect the patient's brain activity.[20]

A Standard for Confirming ALS

Until recently, doctors had no specific list of conditions that defined ALS. They were left to use their judgment in interpreting test results for diagnosing ALS.

In 1998, the World Federation of Neurology (WFN) published a standard that ended the confusion. WFN's Research Group on Motor Neuron Diseases developed El Escorial. This is a scorecard used to tally conditions that must be present to confirm diagnosis of ALS.[21]

El Escorial requires that tests show evidence of both lower and upper motor neuron degeneration. There must be confirmation of progressive spread of symptoms or signs. Tests such as EMG and NCV must confirm motor neuron loss. CT scans and MRI imaging must rule out other diseases.

El Escorial then divides the central nervous system into four regions: the brainstem and the three regions of the spinal cord, which are the cervical (neck); the thoracic (chest); and the lumbosacral (below thoracic). The brainstem involves the jaw, face, palate, tongue, and larynx. Cervical involves the neck, arm, hand, and diaphragm. Thoracic covers back and abdomen. Lumbosacral involves back, abdomen, leg, and foot.

It lists muscle weakness and wasting (atrophy), cramps, and fasciculations as signs of lower motor neuron damage. Signs of upper motor neuron damage include spasticity, slow movement, speech problems, and episodes of uncontrolled laughing or crying.

El Escorial takes much of the guesswork out of diagnosis. It bases certainty on the number of areas of upper and lower motor neurons involved. If three of the four areas of the spinal cord are affected, the diagnosis is "positive." If two areas are involved, the rating will be either "probable" or "possible," depending on the combination of regions involved. If only one lower motor neuron area is involved, there is not enough evidence to confirm that the patient has ALS.

Almost ALS

To make matters even more complicated for the doctor, there are other motor neuron diseases that have some but not all of the markers that distinguish ALS. Primary Lateral Sclerosis, for example, affects only upper motor neurons. Progressive Muscular Atrophy is limited to lower motor neurons. Progressive Bulbar Palsy affects only bulbar muscles. According to El Escorial, they are not ALS.

There are also mimics, such as post-polio syndrome. This condition occurs fifteen or more years after a person had poliomyelitis. The same muscles again weaken and atrophy. Post-polio, however, is easy to distinguish. It does not involve upper motor neurons. In addition, it affects muscles on only one side of the body.[22]

The confusing array of conditions and diseases that mimic ALS frustrates those who treat ALS patients. B.J. Patten, a researcher at the Baylor College of Medicine in the 1980s, was moved to declare that there was no such thing as ALS. "ALS is not a disease," he said. "It is a syndrome suggesting the patient has dysfunction of the lower and upper motor neurons."[23]

Polio and ALS Occurrences

Between 1940 and 1950, two thousand polio cases occurred in Hokkaido, an island in northern Japan. Years later, three hundred eighty-nine cases of ALS developed in this same area. Doctors looked for some connection between the polio and ALS cases. They found a single, strange coincidence—the death rate was higher in ALS patients who had been vaccinated for polio.[24]

Today, research has revealed much more about the disease, but ALS still yields its secrets grudgingly. There is no way to identify who is going to get the disease. No one knows the length of time between ALS onset and its first noticeable signs. There is no warning of its onset. Worse yet, there is no way to identify patients before the damage becomes irreversible.[25]

Once the disease is confirmed, however, the doctor has the burden of telling the patient. In cases involving stroke, heart disease, or even cancer, doctors can offer some hope to their patients. Not so with ALS. The diagnosis doctors most dread to share with patients is to tell them that they have ALS.[26]

6
Searching for a Cure

Ric Shipp was thirty-six years old when he began having trouble swallowing. By profession, the tall African American was an electrician, but he loved sports. He engaged in many activities—softball, football, skating, bike riding, and volleyball.

Shipp knew that he had a lymph node disease called sarcadosis, but then he began to have symptoms that were unrelated to that disease. His speech slurred. He had trouble swallowing. The doctor was even more puzzled when Shipp's tongue began to atrophy.

As the disease progressed, Shipp lost ninety pounds because he had trouble swallowing. In an effort to stop the weight loss, he changed diets. He left out meat, dairy products, and sugar. He ate only whole grain, tofu, fruits, and vegetables. He bought diet supplements at the health store.

Next, he turned to programs that advocated exercise and a positive outlook. After that, he tried cold and hot showers and still more diets. Nothing helped.

Doctors ordered CT scans, MRIs, and spinal taps. Finally, four years into his disease, he had a muscle biopsy done. This showed atrophied nerve fibers consistent with ALS. Suddenly, the score added up. Ric Shipp had ALS.[1]

When he could no longer swallow, Shipp decided to have a feeding tube installed. While in the hospital for this operation, he lost consciousness from lack of oxygen. When he finally left the hospital, he not only had the feeding tube but also a ventilator to breathe.

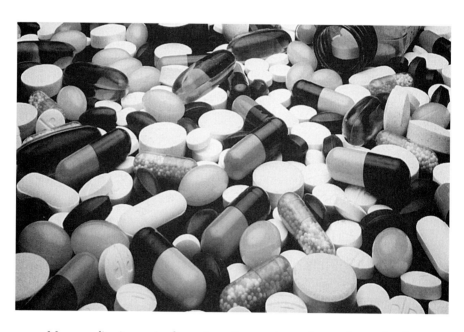

Many medications exist for various diseases, but only one drug, riluzole, has been approved for the treatment of ALS.

Riluzole

Riluzole is the generic name of the only drug approved by the United State Food and Drug Administration (USFDA) for the treatment of ALS. It is manufactured by Rhône Poulenc Rorer. Available since 1996, it is taken in capsule form.[2]

When the experimental drug Myotrophin (mescasermin) became available, he tried that. This drug was designed to restore damaged neurons. Seven months later, he stopped treatment because the injections were too painful.

Next, Shipp tried Rilutek (riluzole). He stopped this medication after three months because he saw no improvement.

Next, Shipp tried a mercury detoxification program. This is based on the theory that dangerous metals cause ALS. The treatment was no more beneficial than the others he had tried.

Shipp's struggle to halt his disease is typical of efforts patients use to control ALS. Many participate in approved drug-testing programs. Others seek benefits from diets, dietary supplements, acupuncture, and even unorthodox remedies and treatments.

Drugs to Treat ALS

Patients are desperate for a drug that will work against ALS or at least give some long-term benefit. So far, only riluzole has been approved, and its effects are very limited. Patients live only a few months longer than they normally would, and there is little improvement in the quality of life.[3]

Research doctor Ralph W. Kuncl likened riluzole to juvenile cancer drugs thirty-five years ago. "We have a drug that works, but not very well."[4]

Mescasermin, the other medication Shipp took, seemed promising, but trials ended in 1999. They showed no clear benefit for patients, and the manufacturer stopped making the drug.[5]

Another drug, Neurontin (gabapentin), has been used to control epilepsy seizures. It helped laboratory mice that had ALS-like symptoms, but had no effect on humans with ALS.[6]

Researchers at Sanofi-Synthelabo conducted studies of its drug called xaliproden. Research on the drug ended in the fall of 2000. Xaliproden proved to be ineffective, as well.[7]

Assessing the Patient's Condition

In order to judge whether a medication is working, researchers look at the patient's condition at the beginning of the trial.

Detoxification

Toxins are deadly substances. When toxin levels are high, the process of removing the poison from the body is called detoxification. This may involve simply avoiding the substance. Or it may mean taking another substance that will neutralize the toxin.

Then they check again at the end of the trial. By comparing the two, they are able to tell whether the drug has helped.

The World Federation of Neurology (WFN) set up an assessment chart in 1996 to determine the patient's condition. This chart, called the ALS Functional Rating Scale, is used worldwide.[8] It rates ten items, such as the ability to speak, swallow, breathe, walk, and climb stairs. It considers handwriting and the ability to feed oneself, dress, turn in bed, and take care of personal hygiene. Each item is scored on a scale that ranges from four (normal) to zero (completely unable to perform task).

The Baylor College of Medicine in Houston, Texas, developed another scale called the Appel ALS Rating Scale.[9] It is named for Dr. Stanley Appel, the chairman of the department of neurology at Baylor. The scale covers the same areas as the one from WFN, but it gives a single, composite score. The Appel scale has been useful in predicting survival time.

Another scale, the Sickness Impact Profile,[10] looks at everyday living. Besides physical factors, it assesses the patient's level of communication, alertness, social interaction, and emotional behavior. It also looks at the patient's ability to participate in home management, work, and recreation.

Researchers use these scales while conducting trials of different medications.

Gauging the Effectiveness of Treatment

Approved trials are carefully controlled. They usually compare the medication against a harmless substitute called a placebo.

One half of the group will get the drug. The other half will get the placebo.

In the case of crossover trials, patients switch at mid-point of the trial. The half getting the placebo then gets the real medication, while the other half gets the placebo. Each group is monitored carefully for results.

Doctors prefer crossover trials, especially for ALS cases. Their patients have such a short time in which to find help. Some doctors consider it unethical to withhold medication that might provide benefit. Patients prefer crossover trials because they know they will get medication at least half the time.

During the trials, patients receiving the placebo sometimes report striking improvement. This happens because they desperately wish to be well. In some cases they do improve, at least for a while. Doctors, however, do not share their optimism. Patients receiving placebos rarely show improvement on the functional rating scales.

Some trials are referred to as "double-blind." In these trials, not even the doctors know who is getting the real medicine. That way, no one can influence the assessment of improvement.

Placebo-based Trials

In a placebo-based trial, half of the patients receive a pill that often contains nothing more than sugar. The placebo has no medicinal value and serves to test whether the real drug works. Patients participating in a placebo-based trial do not know whether they are receiving the true drug or the useless pill.

Fighting Excitotoxicity

Many of the medications being developed for ALS are designed to prevent excitotoxicity. *Excito* means "causing action." *Toxicity* means "poisonous." Excitotoxicity is a condition in which there is too much glutamate.[11]

Glutamate is the neurotransmitter that transfers neuron messages. When a message moves down the axon of the neuron, the terminals of the axon release glutamate. Normally, there is just enough glutamate to carry the impulse across the synapse to stimulate the next neuron. ALS patients, on the other hand, release too much glutamate.

Receptors on the next neuron normally clear the glutamate from the synapse. When there is too much glutamate, it collects in the brain and spinal cord, where it produces calcium. Too much calcium causes neurons to die. Dying neurons then produce more glutamate, and the vicious cycle repeats itself.[12]

Riluzole, the approved medication for ALS, is designed to curb excitotoxicity. It slows down the production of the neurotransmitter.

Dangerous Free Radicals

Free radicals are also enemies of the body. They destroy cells. Some free radicals occur naturally, but disease, poison, and activities like smoking can also generate free radicals.

An example of a free radical is a molecule of oxygen called superoxide. This molecule is short one electron. The natural enemy of this free radical is an enzyme called superoxide

Free Radicals

Molecules normally have an even number of electrons. A free radical has an uneven number. The extra electron causes the free radical to bounce around trying to bond with something. When they bond certain ways, they reproduce themselves in a chain reaction.[13]

dismutase (SOD). SOD causes the free radical to turn into molecules of oxygen and hydrogen peroxide.[14]

One form of SOD, Cu/Zn SOD, contains copper and zinc. Copper is necessary for life, but if it gets into the wrong place in a cell, it causes damage.

In 1999, researchers identified a protein that they believe escorts copper to the correct place in the cell. Researchers suspect that the defective gene on chromosome 21, the one involved in some familial ALS, is allowing free radicals to form when the SOD encounters copper.[15]

Antioxidants

Antioxidants fight free radicals. Health advocates recommend that people eat foods that are high in antioxidants. Antioxidants are those foods that contain vitamins C and E, as well as beta carotene.

Experiments show that high levels of vitamin E, taken before an injury, will help repair the damage. Once the damage is done, however, the vitamin will not repair the body. Lou Gehrig took massive doses of vitamin E with no benefit.[16]

Recently, ALS patients in California took vitamin E as part of a study. They reported that they felt less tired and their muscles did not cramp as much. When the California study was completed, however, it revealed that vitamin E did not repair damaged neurons.[17]

Protecting the Brain

One reason that vitamin E does not work well is that the body will not let it do so. Vitamin E has trouble getting past the blood-brain barrier. To do any good, it must get to the

Blood-Brain Barrier

The brain accounts for only 2 percent of body weight, but it uses 20 percent of the body's blood supply. However, it handles blood differently from other organs. To protect itself, the brain bars certain substances from entering.

To reach the brain, a substance must pass directly through the cell walls of capillaries, the tiny blood vessels that bring blood to cells. Some substances pass through easily, even harmful ones. It takes just ten seconds for nicotine from a cigarette to reach the brain. On the other hand, the blood-brain barrier sometimes turns away substances that may be beneficial, such as vitamin E.[18]

neurons. The body defense system stops that from happening.

Trying to Nourish Neurons

Another problem is that neurons have a built-in code that allows unneeded ones to die. In ALS, unfortunately, they die when they are not supposed to.

Researchers are trying to find neurotrophic factors to help the neurons remain healthy. *Neuro* refers to neurons. *Trophic* means food. Neurotrophic factors are substances that "feed" the neurons. In theory, neurotrophic factors should prevent early neuron death.

One bright factor is the development of laboratory mice that are bred to have ALS-like symptoms. This gives researchers better opportunity to try new medications.

Several types of growth factors have been tested. One kind is an insulin-like growth factor (IGF). It is designed to prevent normal motor neuron death and promote nerve growth. Mescasermin was this type, but it did not work on humans.

Studies of brain-derived neurotrophic factor (BDNF) improved the condition of laboratory mice, but this product did not help humans. Nerve growth factors (NGF) proved ineffective as well.

This variety of efforts prompted Dr. Ralph Kuncl to comment, "What we see coming with neurotrophic factors is the start of an ALS cocktail—the same approach we use for AIDS and cancer—with a variety of drugs, each working at a different point in the process."[19]

Creatine, a Natural Muscle Builder

A natural substance called creatine is another possible candidate to help ALS patients. It occurs in normal cells. In the process of breaking down, it provides energy to make muscles contract.

Health food stores have carried creatine since 1992. Because it is not a drug, anyone can buy it. Athletes take creatine to improve performance. Home run hitter Mark McGwire uses it to build muscles and improve strength. It works in short, intense activity. It does not help, however, with sustained activities such as distance running.[20]

Levels of naturally occurring creatine are very low in both ALS patients and the elderly. Because creatine supplements seemed promising, it was approved for placebo-based trials in three United States ALS clinics.

The problem is that no one knows creatine's long-term effects.

Unusual Treatments

Drug trials often take a year or more. Because patients face a short life expectancy, they do not have the luxury of time. This leads them to try treatments that have no medical proof that they work.

Some people turn to special diets such as vegetables, seaweed, whole brown rice, and liver juice.

Others try to eliminate substances they believe to be dangerous. Excess aluminum is found in Guamanian ALS patients.

81

This has prompted some patients to try to get rid of aluminum. That is almost impossible to do. Aluminum is everywhere—in salt, cheese, antacids, toothpaste, cosmetics, and cooking pots and pans. Some patients have gone so far as to remove dental work that contained aluminum.

Experimental medications have also been tried. Research in the 1970s showed that modified snake venom blocked the action of the polio virus in anterior horn cells. Some ALS patients participated in a double-blind study in which they received modified venom from poisonous cobra and krait snakes. They seemed to improve at first, but the effects did not last.[21]

A doctor who treated boxer Muhammad Ali claimed to have cured an ALS patient using a combination of the drug interferon and the growth hormone Sandostatin. Ali suffers from Parkinson's Disease. There was no proof that the cured patient actually suffered from ALS.[22]

A decade ago, the American Association of Ayurvedic Medicine worked with seven confirmed ALS patients. Ayurvedic medicine, which originated in ancient India, uses herbs mixed in specific proportions. The program included hot oil massages and meditation.[23]

In 1991, a Las Vegas physician claimed to have halted ALS with allergy shots. Because allergy shots are not controlled substances, he conducted no trials and produced no proof that it worked.[24]

More Than One Remedy

It seems likely that no single routine will stop motor neuron loss and promote regrowth. A mixture of medications, vitamins, and supplements is the choice that Steve Shackel made for his treatment.

Shackel is a forty-eight-year-old Australian resident who emigrated from England at the age of fifteen. His interests are wide-ranging. He taught courses in broadcasting and graphic design. He is a

Although not free of ALS symptoms, Steven Shackel is vastly improved from the man first diagnosed with the disease.

former karate champion and still plays the guitar. He is also a licensed handler of venomous snakes.

When Shackel developed ALS in 1994, he began an aggressive fight. He took medicines prescribed by doctors. He changed his diet to include more fruit, vegetables, and grains. He regularly takes a product made from grape seed.

On his Web site, he keeps a running commentary about the steps he has taken and the status of his condition. Amazingly, he has recovered from much of the early weakness. He sent back his wheelchair and now walks without a cane.[25]

Although not free of ALS symptoms, Shackel is vastly improved from the man first diagnosed with the disease. Would his routine work for another patient? Maybe. Maybe not. ALS is too unpredictable to know.

7
Living with ALS

ALS does not have the same timetable for every patient, but, eventually, all patients lose muscle control. One patient described it as a constant state of mourning. Another commented, "You never know what is going to take place tomorrow."[1]

When ALS begins its destructive work, families face a tremendous challenge. Someone must meet the needs of the loved one who is less and less able to perform routine functions. Some families hire helpers to assist the patient, but this is expensive. Many others divide the duties among family members.

Everyone in the family has to adapt to the patient's changing conditions. Some adaptations are simple, but others are expensive and may require special equipment and modifications.

Getting Around

One of the first things many ALS patients have trouble with is walking. The most common cause is foot-drop. The muscles no longer keep the toes pointing forward. When toes drop down, the person trips. A simple plastic brace can prevent foot-drop. The brace slips on the back of the lower leg and keeps the foot at the correct angle.

When a person's gait becomes unsteady, a cane is helpful. These are made of lightweight aluminum, wood, or clear acrylic. Some people feel steadier with a cane that has four small feet.

Some patients use a walker. Wheels make the walker easy to roll. Some patients prefer non-rolling back legs to keep the walker from scooting away. Many walkers have hinged back legs so that they will fold to fit into the car. A bag or basket attached to the walker carries things like a phone, reading material, or the TV remote.

When a wheelchair becomes necessary, it is fitted to the patient. Custom cushions make the chair more comfortable. A battery-powered chair may have a tilting seat and a support for head and neck.

Some patients who still have use of their arms prefer scooter-type wheelchairs. These take up less room and can make turns in tight spaces.

Wheelchairs themselves are expensive. A good, used, manual chair starts at $1,500. A power chair can be more than five times that price. Scooter models run about $4,000. The cost goes up another $1,000 to get a wheelchair lift added to a van.[2]

When a wheelchair becomes necessary, it is fitted to the patient.

Fortunately, Medicare helps with these expenses. ALS clinics and Muscular Dystrophy associations also maintain "loan closets" where patients may borrow equipment.

In the House

Because patients spend so much of their time at home, adjustments help them stay self-sufficient as long as possible. Touch-base lamps require only the slightest contact to turn them on. Speaker phones keep contact between people in different rooms. Electric shavers and toothbrushes require minimal hand movement.

Floor coverings may need to be removed. Loose throw rugs are hazardous. Thick carpets interfere with rolling wheelchairs.

Some house renovations may be necessary to accommodate wheelchairs. Wide doorways and outside ramps provide easy entrance and exit. Bedrooms need to be large enough for free movement. Roll-in showers and higher countertops in bathrooms make personal care much easier.

Bathroom additions include installation of handrails and hand-held shower sprays.

Less expensive bathroom additions include installation of handrails and hand-held shower sprays. Toilet seat extensions and bathing stools help mobile patients get up and down easier.

Some patients have overstuffed chairs with a mechanism that lifts the seat. When the patient presses a button, the seat slowly raises the person to a standing position.

Hospital beds vary the patient's resting positions. Some patients use foam "eggcrate" mattresses, or they have air-filled ones to prevent pressure on body parts.

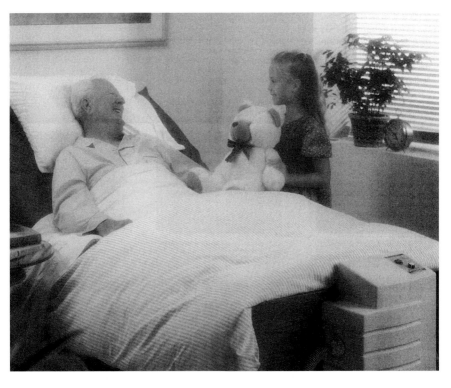

Some patients have air-filled mattresses to prevent pressure on body parts.

Clothing

Wearing larger sizes of clothing is not only comfortable, but the larger armholes make garments easier to get on and off. Hook-and-loop closings such as Velcro work well on shirts and blouses. Pants with elastic waistbands are easier to pull on.

Soft, slip-on shoes work best, but rubber-soled shoes should be avoided. They may cause tripping. Patients find that a long-handled shoehorn helps in putting on shoes.

Eating

ALS patients often have trouble eating. This cuts down on nourishment and causes weight loss. Sometimes, it is a matter of just getting food into the mouth. Wearing wrist splints overcomes some of the lost hand motion.

Utensils have been adapted for patients who have trouble with hand grip. Some have a ring on the handle to slip a finger through. You may see ALS patients eating with an angled spoon or fork. Or they may use a combination spoon and fork called a "spork."

Plastic travel mugs have lids that keep spills to a minimum. Cups and mugs with two handles may be easier to use.

Drinking enough liquids is another problem. Water and other thin liquids spread in the mouth and can go down the windpipe. Adding thickeners makes them easier to swallow. Many patients enjoy frozen ice desserts and fruit juices as a way to increase water intake.

Diets do not need to change, however. But the food must hold together. Otherwise, the patient will choke on small pieces. Moist food such as pudding, gelatin, sauces, fruits, and gravies are the easiest to swallow. Dry foods like bread cause trouble. Even mashed potatoes need lots of gravy to make them go down easily.

Families find that a food blender is their best friend. Sometimes, patients with swallowing problems eat commercial baby food. With a blender, they can have their favorite dishes in a soft consistency.

When a patient's swallowing muscles grow weak, eating becomes a chore. Meals take a long time because the patient has to concentrate on swallowing. Otherwise, food will get into the windpipe.

When choking incidents happen, it is very distressing for the patient and the family. Patients have trouble getting enough breath to cough and clear the airway.

Some patients have learned to cut down on choking episodes by a special food-swallowing routine. The process takes four steps—take a breath and hold it; swallow; exhale; then swallow again.[3]

Getting Enough Oxygen

The same nerve network that controls muscles for swallowing also controls breathing. Weak muscles make it hard to take a deep breath. The diaphragm does not expand the lungs enough to bring in sufficient air.

The time comes, however, when patients cannot swallow enough food to keep them alive. At that point, it is possible to put in a feeding tube that allows nourishment to go directly into the stomach. This is literally a life-or-death situation. The patient can choose whether to have this procedure done.

Breathing

Patients who have trouble breathing find that the problem gets worse when they lie down to sleep. Raising the head of the bed often helps take pressure off the diaphragm. Hospital beds are equipped to do this, but some patients use a folded blanket or extra pillow. In later stages of ALS, patients may sleep sitting up in reclining chairs.

Patients with ALS often develop sleep apnea. While the patients are sleeping, they stop breathing. This can last for a minute or so. Then, the body's alarm system awakens the person. If episodes continue, the lack of oxygen allows carbon dioxide to build up in the blood. Patients suffer headaches and may become confused or drowsy.

One way to combat this lack of oxygen is to use a machine that aids breathing. Before going to bed, patients place a mask over their nose. The mask fits snugly against the face, and the machine pours air into the lungs. When patients get more oxygen, their appetite usually improves.

At the point when breathing muscles fail completely, artificial respirators, or ventilators, are needed to keep oxygen flowing. If the patient has a tracheostomy, a tube is inserted in the throat. This allows a machine to breathe for the patient. Once the tracheostomy tube is in place, however, the patient will no longer be able to speak.

Ventilators and feeding tubes can prolong a patient's life, but some patients choose not to use them. Placing a patient on a ventilator may present the family with an ethical problem. Sometimes, the patient slips into a coma. When that happens, removing the ventilator could be considered as assisted suicide, which is illegal in most states.

Speech

Words begin to slur when throat and mouth muscles can no longer form the correct shapes. Finally, though, patients cannot speak at all. For many, losing the ability to speak is the hardest thing they must bear.[4]

Patients who cannot speak may work out a card system in which they point to letters or phrases. Some patients who can still move their hands learn American Sign Language. Those without hand movement work out a system of blinks to communicate.

It takes a lot of patience to work at such a slow pace, but Howard Hornstein, a Connecticut dentist, had such persistence. He loved to sing old sea chanteys. When his ALS worsened, he gave up his practice but not his friends and the songs they sang.

Using an attachment on his glasses, Hornstein wrote a book using only his right eye. His eye scanned letters of the alphabet. When his eye stopped moving, the attachment

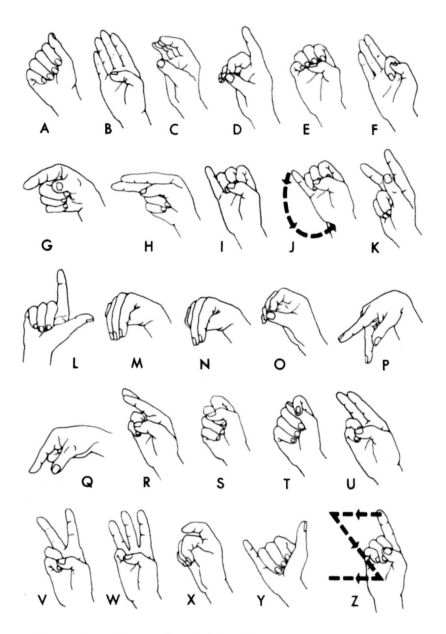

Some patients who can still use their hands learn American Sign Language.

sent the letter to his computer. It took him two years to write *Sea Songs*.[5]

A Team Effort

Many types of professionals are involved in the care of an ALS patient. Neurologists monitor the patient's physical condition. Speech therapists show patients how to substitute sounds when speech slurs. Occupational therapists teach ways to cope with everyday routines such as eating and dressing. Home health aides arrive to help with routines such as bathing.

Physical therapists work to conserve muscle strength. Physical exercise can not rebuild muscle that has been lost through ALS. In fact, too much exercise simply uses energy the patient needs for other activities.

The goal is to keep limbs moving. Range-of-motion exercises can be done with patients even after they can no longer move their arms and legs themselves.

High Costs

The financial costs associated with ALS are high. Caring for an ALS patient in advanced stages of the disease costs approximately $200,000 a year.[6]

Medications are expensive, and many hospital plans do not cover treatments. Fortunately, in December 2000, Congress lifted the 24-month waiting period for Medicare coverage for ALS patients.[7]

Beyond the financial costs are the costs in human terms. Meeting the needs of an ALS patient is both time-consuming and emotionally draining.

Sometimes neighbors and friends help. They prepare meals, exercise the patient's muscles, or provide breaks for family members. Ultimately, though, the job falls to the primary caregiver.

As the disease progresses, the caregiver assumes full responsibility for the patient's day-to-day physical needs. Caregivers help patients walk or transfer to chair, bed, or car. They exercise muscles, cook meals, drive cars, push wheelchairs, and help with daily hygiene.

In addition, they anticipate the patient's needs. They understand speech that others cannot recognize. When the patient can no longer talk, they figure out what the patient wants.

In spite of problems involved in home care, many doctors feel that relatives and friends can be trained to provide home care for the severely disabled.[8]

Caregivers have a heavy responsibility, but they have a reason to do what they are doing. One caregiver summed it up by saying, "For me, it is a lot of responsibility with a lot of rewards. It is a chance to outwardly express my respect and love for my husband."[9]

Finding Support and Comfort

Both patients and their families find emotional support and practical advice at local associations for ALS. At meetings,

ALS Caregivers

Caregivers face a challenge in caring for ALS patients. One researcher identified five stages that caregivers go through:

1. "Taking it"—They are aware that ALS is an uncontrollable event.

2. "Staying afloat"—They are tolerating inconveniences and trying to keep things normal.

3. "Losing ground"—They have lost relationships, privacy, and even tolerance.

4. "Regrouping"—They regain control with outside assistance, either physical or spiritual. They are successful, even if only temporarily.

5. "Holding together"—They are doing what they can, accepting and adjusting to what comes.[10]

patients and caregivers find others who are struggling with the same problems.

Many find comfort in their religious faith. Patients know their time is limited and gain a new attitude about what is important. Many learn to live in the present and to appreciate what they have. One commented, "I still feel like I've won the lottery by marrying Laura and having two great kids. I don't cry about what I don't have anymore."[11]

8

Facing the Future

Morrie Schwartz sat in the glare of the television cameras. He talked to ABC newsman Ted Koppel about his approaching death. Instead of being bitter, the retired sociology professor focused on his philosophy of life.

Sportswriter Mitch Albom heard that broadcast and recognized his college mentor. He knew he had to have more time with this remarkable man. For weeks, he flew from Chicago to Boston every Tuesday to listen to his teacher. The lessons he learned about living are recorded in *Tuesdays with Morrie.*

Albom's book was published in 1997. It became a perennial bestseller because it made people think about things that are really important in life. A made-for-TV movie based on the book starred Jack Lemmon. It won three awards at the 2000 Emmy presentations.

Tuesdays With Morrie made the public think about dying with dignity. Bill and Judith Moyers, acclaimed television producers, explored that subject in a four-part documentary. PBS aired "On Our Own Terms" in September 2000.

One of the persons profiled in the documentary was an ALS patient. The woman knew everything that was going on, but she could move only her eyes.

ALS patients know that they face a bleak future. Some terminally ill patients have chosen suicide as a way out of the situation. In 1998, CBS carried a program showing Dr. Jack Kevorkian helping an ALS patient to die.

The broadcast brought a storm of protest. The network quickly presented a program featuring other ALS patients. Their wide-ranging interests showed a fierce will to live. Dan Beacombe summed it up by saying, "You can find something good every day."[1]

Stephen Hawking is proof that the disease does not mean the end of accomplishments. Hawking, a professor at Cambridge University in England, has lived with the disease longer than anybody else. He has had it for nearly forty years. In spite of the disease, he is known world-wide both as a scientist and an ALS survivor.

Born in 1942, Hawking developed ALS as a college student. After the initial shock of learning that his disease was incurable, he decided to live with what he had. He took a teaching job, married, and eventually had three children. He is now a grandfather.

Hawking is noted for his ideas about time and space. He also wrote a bestseller for laypeople called *A Brief History of Time.*

For more than fifteen years, Hawking has required round-the-clock care. In spite of that, he continues to teach and write. He travels and lectures around the world.

Hawking uses the one finger he can still move to tap keys on the computer attached to his wheelchair. To speak, he sends the words from the computer to a speech synthesizer.

Hawking firmly believes that "one need not lose hope."[2]

Renowned astrophysicist Stephen Hawking demonstrates his new notebook computer, specially modified for him by Intel engineers, for then Intel chairman Gordon Moore at Cambridge University.

Research Funding

One of the reasons for hope is that research is getting closer to discovering a cure for ALS.

The United States government supports medical research through the National Institutes of Health (NIH). One part of NIH is the National Institute of Neurological Disorders and Stroke (NINDS).

NINDS focuses on cause, diagnosis, treatment, and prevention of neurological diseases. Its budget for 2000 was nearly $891,000,000. These funds provide for the study of disorders such as ALS, Parkinson's, Alzheimer's, multiple sclerosis, stroke, and brain tumors.[3]

Part of the NINDS funding is used for orphan drugs that treat rare diseases. ALS, although not truly rare, is classed in this category.

Often, pharmaceutical companies will not make a drug without government money for its manufacture. This frustrates patients who wish to have the medication.

Research funded by the government is restricted as well. Stem cell research, for example, is legal only if done with

Orphan Drugs

Orphan drugs are ones that will not sell in large quantities because relatively few patients need them. In exchange for providing the drugs, pharmaceutical companies receive special tax advantages to help cover the cost of manufacture.

Stem Cells

Stem cells are embryonic cells that can develop into any type cell. They are found in human embryos. The umbilical cord, discarded after birth, is one source of stem cells.

private funds.[4] ALS researchers are hopeful that stem cells can be used to replace damaged neurons.

The families of ALS patients are eager to speed up the research on the disease. This has led private foundations to raise money to conduct research that will not limited by government guidelines.

The family of New York actress Jenifer Estress organized such a foundation. Their high profile has brought large donations for research not bound by government regulations.[5]

Another private organization, the Les Turner ALS Foundation, honoring a Chicago businessman, has been heavily involved in research, but it goes beyond that. The foundation sponsors many activities. It also provides clinic services for patients and their families.[6]

Other organizations are more grassroots. Ride for Life seeks to make legislators aware of the need to fund ALS research. Each year, a group of ALS patients and their caregivers ride to Washington, D.C. in wheelchairs. Their arrival is timed to coincide with ALS Advocacy Day.

The first "Ride for Life" was organized in 1998 by ALS patient Chris Pendergast, a teacher from Long Island. They left from Yankee Stadium in New York City on a 350-mile trek that took fifteen days.

Ride for Life's Website records events and research related to ALS. It also features profiles of ALS patients. The organization's modest fundraising provides free respite care and some legal services to families of ALS patients.[7]

Mark Reiman, an ALS patient, made a personal crusade of raising public awareness of his disease. During the 1998 baseball season, the Seattle, Washington, resident achieved a personal goal. He sang the national anthem in all thirty major league ball parks.[8]

The national clearinghouse for ALS information is the ALS Association (ALSA). This major organization not only funds research, but also seeks to improve the quality of life for those living with ALS. It has affiliates in many states.

Over the past decade, ALSA has supplied millions of dollars for research to find a cure for ALS. Its newest project is an aggressive program called the Lou Gehrig Fund. Part of the fund will focus on using information from the Human Genome Project.

The Human Genome Project still has much work to be done. The gene sequence of "letters" is known, but it will take years to understand how these work. "We've got our instruction book," said James Watson, one of discoverers of the structure of DNA. But, he added, "We can't read it all yet."[9]

Human Genome Project

In 2000, scientists announced that they had all but completed mapping the genes in the body. Researchers have recorded the 3.1 billion chemical "letters" that make up human DNA. They expect this information to reveal the genes that trigger certain diseases.[10]

On the Verge of Success

Other types of research explore whether cells grown in the laboratory can replace damaged tissue. Others test gene therapy as a way to replace defective genes. Several groups focus on ways to eliminate excessive glutamate that kills motor neurons.

Dr. Hiroshi Mitsumoto, Chairman of ALSA's Medical Advisory Committee, is optimistic about conquering ALS. He cites several factors that are already in place. One of them is the discovery of the defective gene that is linked to some cases of familial ALS. Dr. Mitsumoto believes that we are on the verge of even more exciting discoveries.[11]

Dr. Stanley Appel of the Baylor College of Medicine agrees. While appearing on a Houston, Texas, TV talk show, he commented on the advances made in treating ALS. "We are close enough to tell people to do what they want to do today."[12]

Researchers are optimistic that ALS will soon lose its designation as a fatal disease.

Q&A

Q. Why is ALS called "Lou Gehrig's Disease?"

A. The common name in the United States is that of the great Yankee baseball player, Lou Gehrig. He died of ALS in 1941. His popularity made the public aware of the disease.

Q. Can I catch ALS from someone else?

A. No, ALS is not contagious. Most cases occur randomly.

Q. Will performing certain exercises prevent ALS?

A. Exercising will not prevent ALS, nor does it help once the disease starts.

Q. A family I know has several cases of ALS. How did they get it?

A. About 10 percent of ALS cases are inherited. In a small percent of these, a defective gene has been identified as a trigger for getting the disease.

Q. How will I know if I have the mutant gene?

A. There are tests to determine this.

Q. Is ALS like Alzheimer's Disease?

A. No, ALS does not affect the mind. It affects muscles, but only certain ones. It does not affect the eyes nor any of the senses.

Q. Do young people get ALS?

A. There are far fewer cases of ALS among young people than among people who are over fifty-five.

Q. Do certain parts of the world have more cases of ALS?

A. ALS can occur anywhere, but it is found more often in temperate climates. A small group of people living in areas of the Pacific have the Guamanian form of ALS.

Q. Can living near power lines or exposure to lead paint make me more likely to get ALS?

A. Studies conducted so far have made no connection.

Q. Does food have anything to do with ALS?

A. It is always wise to have a healthy diet, but there is no known connection with food. Patients can eat any food they like, but eventually the disease makes it impossible for them to swallow.

ALS Timeline

1700 B.C.—Edwin Smith Surgical Papyrus was written, which gave a visual description of the brain.

100 A.D.—Rufus of Ephesus published *On the Names of the Parts of the Human Body*, showing the connection between brain and nerves.

177—Galen, a native of Pergamum, lectured on the brain and described what happened when he cut the spinal cord in monkeys.

1543—Andreas Vesalius published *On the Workings of the Human Body*, in which he showed nerves running from the brain throughout the body.

1717—Anton van Leeuvenhoek observed a cross-section of a nerve fiber.

1791—Luigi Galvani published information about electrical stimulation of frog nerves.

1836—Robert Remak described a myelinated fiber.

1844—Remak illustrated the 6-layered cortex of the brain.

1865—Otto Friedrich Karl Deiters explained that dendrites receive messages.

1877—Jean-Martin Charcot published *Lectures on the Diseases of the Nervous System*.

1889—Santiago Ramon y Cajal stated that nerve cells do not touch when they pass messages.

1891—Wilhelm von Waldeyer coined the term "neuron" and showed how nerves worked together to pass messages.

1897—Charles Scott Sherrington coined the term "synapse."

1906—Camillo Golgi and Ramon Y Cajal earned the Nobel Prize for explaining the structure of the nervous system.

1941—Lou Gehrig died of ALS.

1993—Researchers identified a mutant gene on chromosome 21 that triggers familial ALS.

1996—Rilutek (riluzole) was made available by prescription.

2001—Human genome mapping was completed.

Glossary

antioxidant—A vitamin or food component that combats free radicals.

atrophy—A condition where muscles waste away.

axon—The nerve fiber that carries messages to the next neuron.

blood-brain barrier—A defense in which the capillaries carrying blood keep substances from reaching the brain.

brainstem—The downward extension of the brain that joins the spinal cord.

bulbar onset—The start of ALS in the bulbar (widened) part of the brainstem.

capillary—The thin wall of the blood vessel through which oxygen and other substances pass from the blood into tissue.

chromosome—A threadlike structure in the cell nucleus that carries genetic information.

cortex—The thin outer layer of the cerebrum where thought and action are generated.

dendrite—The bushy ends of a nerve cell through which messages are received.

DNA (deoxyribonucleic acid)—The arrangement of genetic material that controls heredity and makes us each individual.

excitotoxicity—The poisonous state in which too much glutamate causes neurons to die.

fasciculations—The uncontrolled twitching of muscles.

free radicals—A highly unstable molecule with an extra electron that makes it seek out other molecules with which to bond.

genome—The total genetic material in an individual. The human genome has twenty-three pairs of chromosomes.

glutamate—A neurotransmitter that carries messages across the synapse between motor neurons.

gyrus—The hump between a groove (sulcus), part of the "wrinkled" effect on the brain's surface.

hyperreflexia—Overreaction of a muscle when a tendon is tapped.

involuntary muscle—A muscle over which we have no conscious control.

lateral—To the side.

limb onset—The state in which ALS symptoms first occur in the arms or legs.

lower motor neuron—Neurons that run from the spinal cord to the muscle.

myelin—The shiny coating on some nerve fibers.

neuron—The combination of a nerve cell and its fiber.

neurotransmitter—The substance that carries impulses across the synapse between neurons.

nerve fiber—The long projection from a nerve cell down which the impulse travels.

nucleus—The cell body; the part of a cell that contains genetic material (DNA).

plaque—An obstructing foreign substance.

placebo—A harmless substitute for medicine used in drug trials.

protein—An organic compound of carbon, hydrogen, oxygen, and nitrogen essential to the human body.

receptors—The place on the dendrites that receives the neurotransmitter.

sclerosis—Hardening.

sleep apnea—A condition in which a person stops breathing while asleep.

spasticity—The rigidity of muscles due to both sets of opposing muscles being in tension.

sporadic—Random.

sulcus—A groove in the brain, as opposed to the gyrus.

symmetry—The state of having both sides the same.

synapse—The space between neurons across which impulses pass.

toxin—A poison.

tracheostomy—A procedure that opens a hole in the windpipe, formerly called tracheotomy.

tumor—An abnormal growth.

upper motor neuron—Neuron that runs between the brain and the spinal cord.

ventilator—A machine that breathes for a person.

voluntary muscles—Muscles that we can consciously control.

wasting—Atrophy.

For More Information

The ALS Association National Office
27001 Agoura Road, Suite 150
Calabasas Hills, CA 91301
(800) 782-4747
alsinfo@alsa-national.org.
http://www.alsa.org

International Alliance of ALS/MND Associations
on the Internet:
http://www.alsmndalliance.org

International ALS Organizations:
ALS Society of Canada
6 Adelaide Street East, Suite 220
Toronto, Ontario M5C 1H6
Canada
(416) 362-0414
alssoc@inforamp.net

Les Turner ALS Foundation
8142 N. Lawndale Avenue
Skokie, IL 60076
(708) 679-3311
http://www.lesturnerals.org

Motor Neurone Disease Association of the United Kingdom
P. O. Box 246
Northampton, NN1 2PR, UK
01 44 1604 250505

A list of **U.S. Certified ALSA Clinical Care Centers** is
available at http://www.alsa.org/Services/

Chapter Notes

Chapter 1. Lou Gehrig: Great Man, Terrible Disease

1. "Lou Gehrig's Farewell Speech," <http://www.nmia.com/~browns/gehrig5.htm> (November 1, 1999).

2. "The Iron Horse: a Tribute to Lou Gehrig," <http://www.nmia.com/~browns/gehrig.htm> (November 1, 1999).

3. "Hunter Dead of Gehrig's Disease," *Houston Chronicle*, September 10, 1999; Melissa August, et al, "Eulogy," *Time*, June 14, 1999, p. 41.; James Wynbrandt and Mark D. Ludman, *The Encyclopedia of Genetic Disorders and Birth Defects* (New York: Facts on File, 1991), p. 23.; Loren A. Rolak, ed., *Neurology Secrets*, 2nd ed. (Philadelphia: Hanley & Belfers, 1988), p. 92; Frazier Moore, "Soap Actor's Illness Brings Realism to 'One Life to Live'," Associated Press, May 11, 1998, <http://www.rideforlife.com/ppzaz.htm> (June 2, 1999); "The ALS Association Mourns the Loss of Actor Michael Zaslow," <http://www.alsa.org/News/michaelzaslow.html> (April 7, 1999).

Chapter 2. ALS—History of a Puzzle

1. "What Is ALS?," <http://www.bcm.tmc.edu/neurol/struct/als/als7a.html> (April 12, 1999).

2. Edwin Clarke and C. D. O'Malley, *The Human Brain and Spinal Cord: a Historical Study Illustrated by Writings from Antiquity to the Twentieth Century* (Berkeley: University of California Press, 1968), p. 384.

3. "The Edwin Smith Surgical Papyrus; the first use of 'neuro' words in recorded history," <http://faculty.washington.edu/chudler/papy.html> (August 5, 2000); Robert H. Wilkins, "Neurosurgical Classic-XVII-Edwin Smith Surgical Papyrus," <http://www.neurosurgery.org/pubpages/cybermuseum/pre20th/epapyrus.html> (August 5, 2000).

4. Clarke, p. 3; Susan A. Greenfield, *The Human Brain, A Guided Tour* (New York: BasicBooks, 1997).

5. Ibid.

6. "Milestones in Neuroscience Research," <http://faculty.washington.edu/chudler/hist.html> (August 5, 2000).

7. Clarke, p. 13.

8. Galen, *Anatomical Procedures*, IX, 13-14, as quoted in Clarke, p. 292.

9. "Milestones in Neuroscience Research," Greenfield, p. 68; Walther Riese, *A History of Neurology* (New York: MD Publications, 1959), p. 191.

10. Clarke, p. 46.

11. "Milestones in Neuroscience Research."

12. Clarke, p. 51.

13. "Milestones in Neuroscience Research."

14. Ibid.

15. "Milestones in Neuroscience Research."

16. Ibid.

17. Clarke, p. 239.

18. "Milestones in Neuroscience Research."

19. Clarke, p. 114.

20. Robert J. Watson, "Jean Martin Charcot," *International Encyclopedia of the Social Sciences*, vol. 2 (New York: The Macmillan Co. & The Free Press, 1968), pp. 384–386.

21. Robert C. Collins, *Neurology* (Philadelphia: W. B. Saunders Co., 1997), p. 118.

22. Watson, pp. 384–386.

23. Andrew Eisen and Charles Krieger, *Amyotrophic Lateral Sclerosis: A Synthesis of Research and Clinical Practice* (Cambridge: University Press, 1998), p. 29.

Chapter 3. Movement—Brain to Muscle

1. Bobbye Lott, author interview, October 28, 1999.

2. Susan A. Greenfield, *The Human Brain, A Guided Tour* (New York: BasicBooks, 1997), p. 5.

3. Ibid., p. 15.

4. "Brain Facts and Figures," <http://faculty.washington.edu/chudler/facts.html> (September 4, 2000).

5. Alvin Silverstein and Virginia Silverstein, *World of the Brain* (New York: William Morrow and Co., 1986), p. 13.

6. Greenfield, p. 78.

7. Edwin Clarke and C. D. O'Malley, *The Human Brain and Spinal Cord: a Historical Study Illustrated by Writings from Antiquity to the Twentieth Century* (Berkeley: University of California Press, 1968), p. 115.

8. Greenfield, p. 37; Andrew Eisen and Charles Krieger, *Amyotrophic Lateral Sclerosis: A Synthesis of Research and Clinical Practice* (Cambridge: University Press, 1998), p. 163.

9. Eisen, p. 28.

10. *Harrison's Principals of Internal Medicine* (New York: McGraw-Hill, Inc., 1994), p. 2281.

Chapter 4. What Is ALS?

1. Linda Gibson, "One Door Closed—Others Opened: Marcie Gibson's Story," <http://www.rideforlife.com/pp_marcie_gibson.htm> (June 2, 1999); Linda Gibson, "Shattered Dreams," *ALS Association Newsletter North Texas Chapter*, Arlington, Texas, May 2000, p. 1–2.

2. "What Is ALS?," <http://www.alsa.org/What Is/> (April 7, 1999).

3. Andrew Eisen and Charles Krieger, *Amyotrophic Lateral Sclerosis: A Synthesis of Research and Clinical Practice* (Cambridge: University Press, 1998), p. 35.

4. Hiroshi Mitsumoto and Forbes H. Norris, *Amyotrophic Lateral Sclerosis: A Comprehensive Guide to Management* (New York: Demos Publications, 1994), pp. 2–3.

5. Eisen, p. 1.

6. Karl E. Misulis, *Essentials of Clinical Neurophysiology,* 2nd ed. (Boston: Butterworth-Heinemann, 1997), p. 259.

7. "What Is ALS?," <http://www.alsa.org/What Is/>.

8. "International Alliance of ALS/MND Associations on the Internet" <http://www.alsmndalliance.org> (September 15, 2000).

9. Eisen, p. 10.

10. Robin Balsdon, "Enjoying Life—One Neurone at a Time," <http://www.rideforlife.com/pp_robin_balsdon.htm> (June 2, 1999).

11. Walther Riese, *A History of Neurology* (New York: MD Publications, 1959), p. 198.

12. Megan Rutherford, "A Teacher's Last Lesson: Her Incurable Illness is a Powerful Classroom Tool," Time, June 5, 2000, p. 60.

13. "What Is ALS?," <http://www.alsa.org/What Is/>.

14. Mitsumoto, p. 4.

15. Eisen, p. 26: "Amyotrophic Lateral Sclerosis Fact Sheet" <http://www.ninds.nih.gov/health_and_medical/pubs/als.htm> (March 28, 2001).

16. Al Picken, "Generations of ALS: A Personal History," <http://www.premier1.net/~dusta/myals.htm> (May 8, 1999).

17. "What Is ALS?" <http://www.alsa.org/What Is/>.

18. "What Causes ALS?" <http://www.bcm.tmc.edu/neurol/struct/als/als7e.html> (April 12, 1999).

19. Eisen, p. 109.

20. Mitsumoto, pp. 4–5.

21. Eisen, p. 20.

22. Ibid., p. 109.

23. Ibid., p. 21.

24. Ibid., p. 20.

25. Ibid.

26. Ibid., pp. 20–21.

27. Ibid., p. 22.

28. "New Hope for People with ALS," *FDA Consumer*, September 1996, as quoted in *Brain Disorders Sourcebook* (Detroit, Michigan: Omnigraphics, Inc., 1999), p. 258.

29. Mitsumoto, p. 5.

Chapter 5. Diagnosing ALS

1. Andrew Eisen and Charles Krieger, *Amyotrophic Lateral Sclerosis: A Synthesis of Research and Clinical Practice* (Cambridge: University Press, 1998), p. 29.

2. "Fascicle," *The Bantam Medical Dictionary*, 2nd revised ed. (New York: Books, 1994), p. 166.

3. Eisen, p. 55.

4. Hiroshi Mitsumoto and Forbes H. Norris, *Amyotrophic Lateral Sclerosis: A Comprehensive Guide to Management* (New York: Demos Publications, 1994), pp. 10–11.

5. Ibid., p. 8.

6. Charles B. Clayman, ed., *The Brain and Nervous System* (New York: Dorling Kindersley, Ltd. and American Medical Association, 1991), p. 30.

7. "Plantar reflex," *The Bantam Medical Dictionary*, p. 350.

8. Eisen, p. 31.

9. Mitsumoto, p. 8.

10. "Milestones in Neuroscience Research."

11. "Laboratory Tests and Procedures," <http://www.bcm.tmc.edu/neurol/struct/als/als7d2.html> (May 17, 1999).

12. Ibid.

13. Ibid.

14. Ibid.

15. "Muscle Biopsy," <http://www.bcm.tmc.edu/neurol/struct/als/als7d4.html> (May 17, 1999).

16. "Electrodiagnostic Tests," <http://www.bcm.tmc.edu/neurol/struct/als/als7d1.html> (May 17, 1999); Eisen, pp. 150,189.

17. Ibid.

18. "X-ray and imaging studies," <http://www.bcm.tmc.edu/neurol/struct/als/als7d3.html> (May 17, 1999).

19. Susan A. Greenfield, *The Human Brain, A Guided Tour* (New York: BasicBooks, 1997), pp. 26–31.

20. Alvin Silverstein and Virginia Silverstein, *World of the Brain* (New York: William Morrow and Co., 1986), p. 106.

21. "Revised Criteria for the Diagnosis of Amyotrophic Lateral Sclerosis," <http://www.wfnals.org/Articles/elescorial1998criteria.htm> (April 7, 1999).

22. Mitsumoto, p. 5.

23. V. Cosi, et al, eds., *Amyotrophic Lateral Sclerosis: Therapeutic, Psychological and Research Aspects.* Proceedings of an International Congress on Therapeutic, Psychological and Research Aspects of Amyotrophic Lateral Sclerosis, held March 27–31, 1985, at Villa Ponti, Varese, Italy (New York: Plenum Press, 1987), pp. 106–107.

24. Eisen, p. 19.

25. Ibid., pp. 31, 209.

26. Loren A. Rolak, ed., *Neurology Secrets*, 2nd ed. (Philadelphia: Hanley & Belfers, 1988), p. 386.

Chapter 6. Searching For a Cure

1. Ric Shipp, "PALS Profiles: Stories of people living with ALS," <http://www.rideforlife.com/pp_shipp060199.htm> (June 2, 1999).

2. "Rilutek (riluzole) Now Available by Prescription for ALS" <http://www.pslgroup.com/dg/604e.htm> (April 7, 1999).

3. Andrew Eisen and Charles Krieger, *Amyotrophic Lateral Sclerosis: A Synthesis of Research and Clinical Practice* (Cambridge: University Press, 1998), p. 221.

4. "New drug with unusual promise enters ALS pipeline," <http://www.lougehrigsdisease.net/als_news/990706new_drug_with_unusual_promise_en.htm> (August 17, 1999).

5. Mariam Uhlman and Lisa Fine, "Why Did Cephalon Drop Myotrophin," *Philadelphia Inquirer*, December 22, 1999, <http://www.rideforlife.com/n_myotrophin122499.htm> (December 24, 1999).

6. "Researchers Sadly Report Neurontin Is a Failure, Drug Does Nothing to Stop Progression of ALS," <http://www.rideforlife.com/n_neurontin101399.htm> (October 13, 1999).

7. "Sanofi-Synthalebo Releases Preliminary Analysis for Xaliproden," <http://www.alsa.org/news/news090500.cfm> (September 9, 2000).

8. "The Amyotrophic Lateral Sclerosis Functional Rating Scale (ALSFRS)," <http://www.wfnals.org/Articles/ALSFRS.htm> (April 7, 1999).

9. "Quantitative Disease Progression Study (Appel ALS Rating Scale)," <http://www.bcm.tmc.edu/neurol/struct/als/als9.html> (April 12, 1999).

10. Eisen, p. 214.

11. Ibid. p. 231.

12. "Synthetic Steroid Dramatically Reduces Stroke Damage," <http://www.pslgroup.com/dg/39652.htm> (May 7, 1999).

13. "Radical, free," *Tabor's Cyclopedic Medical Dictionary* (Philadelphia: F.A. Davis Company, 1985), p. 1550.

14. "Superoxide" and "superoxide dismutase," Tabor's, p. 1783.

15. Alison Davis, "Heavy Metal Research is Music to Biologists' Ears," <http://www.nih.gov/nigms/news/releases/copper.html> (November 12, 1999).

16. Eisen, p. 216.

17. V. Cosi, et al, eds., *Amyotrophic Lateral Sclerosis: Therapeutic, Psychological and Research Aspects.* Proceedings of an International Congress on Therapeutic, Psychological and Research Aspects of Amyotrophic Lateral Sclerosis, held March 27–31, 1985, at Villa Ponti, Varese, Italy (New York: Plenum Press, 1987), p. 184.

18. Susan A. Greenfield, *The Human Brain, A Guided Tour* (New York: BasicBooks, 1997), p. 83.

19. Kuncl, as reported in "New drug with unusual promise enters ALS pipeline."

20. "Researchers: No problems found with creatine but. . . " <http://www.lougehrigsdisease.net/als_news/009605researchers.htm> (August 17, 1999).

21. Hiroshi Mitsumoto and Forbes H. Norris, *Amyotrophic Lateral Sclerosis: A Comprehensive Guide to Management* (New York: Demos Publications, 1994), p. 54.

22. Ibid., p. 57

23. Ibid., p. 58

24. Ibid., p. 60.

25. Steven Shackel, "My Story," <goulburn.net.au/~shack/history.htm> (November 4, 1999).

Chapter 7. Living with ALS

1. Harry Moore, *Debra Duncan Show*, ABC Channel 13, Houston, Texas, July 10, 2000.

2. Lark of America; Dean Floyd, May 2, 2000.

3. V. Cosi, et al, eds., *Amyotrophic Lateral Sclerosis: Therapeutic, Psychological and Research Aspects.* Proceedings of an International Congress on Therapeutic, Psychological and Research Aspects of Amyotrophic Lateral Sclerosis, held March 27–31, 1985, at Villa Ponti, Varese, Italy (New York: Plenum Press, 1987), p. 205.

4. Michael Toennis, *Debra Duncan Show* (July 10, 2000).

5. Mary Voboril, "Howard's Song—A bold man and the sea: Life with ALS still sings with joy," Newsday, Inc., 1998, <http://www.rideforlife.com/pp_hornstein.htm> (September 28, 1999).

6. "What is ALS?" <http://www.alsa.org/What Is/> (March, 2001).

7. "Congress Waives 24-month Medicare Waiting Period," <http://www.alsa.org/new121500b.cfm> (January 24, 2001).

8. Cosi, p. 237.

9. Cindy Tewes, "Patient/Family Closeups," interview, <http://www.alsa.org/als/cu_tewes.cfm> (September 15, 2000).

10. Hiroshi Mitsumoto and Forbes H. Norris, *Amyotrophic Lateral Sclerosis: A Comprehensive Guide to Management* (New York: Demos Publications, 1994), p. 242.

11. Russ Daughtry, as quoted in Lisa Stein, "Russ Daughtry: Musician's Spirit Still Sings Out Despite ALS," *Chicago Tribune*, June 1, 1999, <http://www.rideforlife.com/pp_daughtry060199 .htm> (June 2, 1999).

Chapter 8. Facing the Future

1. "60 Minutes Transcript: Choosing life; patients with ALS, Lou Gehrig's disease, tell of their love and passion for life, even while their bodies continue to fail them," February 28, 1999, CBS, Inc., <http://www.rideforlife.com/n_60mintrans030499.htm> (April 8, 1999).

2. "A Brief History of Mine," <http://www.hawking.org.uk/ about/aindex.html (September 11, 2000).

3. "Testimony of Gerald Fischbach," Statement of the Director, National Institute of Neurological Disorders and Stroke, before Congress of the United States, February 23, 1999, as reported in <http://www.rideforlife.com/n_ninds022500.htm> (April 8, 1999).

4. Kevin Murphy, "Senate Panel Hears Debate on Funding for Stem Cell Research," *Kansas City Star*, September 15, 2000, <http:// www.rideforlife.com/n_stemcell091500.htm> (September 15, 2000).

5. Wadler, Joyce, "Immobilized, and Energized, by an Illness," *The New York Times*, January 27, 1999, <http://www.rideforlife .com/n_estess012899.htm> (June 2, 1999).

6. Les Turner Amyotrophic Lateral Sclerosis Foundation, Ltd., <http://www.lesturnals.org/> (April 17, 1999).

7. "What is the Ride for Life?" <http://www.rideforlife.com /ride98.htm> (April, 1999); "Ride for Life 2000" <http://www .rideforlife.com/ride2000_index.htm> (September 11, 2000).

8. "Michael Booth, "National Anthem Crooner Sings of Strength: ALS Patient Tours US Ballparks," *Denver Post*, May 5, 1998, <http://www.rideforlife.com/ppmark.htm> (September 15, 2000; "The ALS Association Presents its Inaugural Voice of Courage Award to USA Today Correspondent," <http://www.alsa.org/news/news051900.cfm> (September 9, 2000).

9. Aaron Zitner and Richard Saltus, "Reading the Human Genome Key to Cures," *The Boston Globe*, September 26, 1999, <http://www.rideforlife.com/rr_genome100199.htm> (July 10, 2000).

10. Michael D. Lemonick, "The Genome is Mapped. Now What?" *Time*, July 3, 2000, p. 24-29.

11. Hiroshi Mitsumoto, "Understanding ALS," <http://www.alsa.org/als/whatis.cfm> (September 11, 2000).

12. Stanley Appel, *Debra Duncan Show* (July 10, 2000).

Further Reading

Endelson, Edward. *The Nervous System*. New York: Chelsea House Publishers, 1989.

Macht, Norman L. *Lou Gehrig*. New York: Chelsea House Publishers, 1992.

Mitsumoto, Hiroshi, and Theodore Munsat. *Amyotrophic Lateral Sclerosis: A Guide for Patients and Families*. New York: Demos Medical Publishing, Inc., 2001.

Parker, Steve. *Brain and Nerves*. Brookfield, Connecticut: Copper Beech Books, 1998.

Rabin, Roni. *Six Parts Love: A Family's Battle with Lou Gehrig's Disease (ALS)*. New York: Simon & Schuster Trade, 1985.

Silverstein, Alvin, Robert Silverstein, and Virginia Silverstein. *The Nervous System*. New York: Twenty-First Century Books, 1995.

Internet Addresses

ALS Association
<http://www.alsa.org>

ALS Survival Guide
<http://lougehrigsdisease.net>

Professor Stephen Hawking's Homepage
<http://www.hawking.org.uk>

Ride for Life
<http://www.rideforlife.com>

Steven Shackel
<http://www.goulburn.net.au/~shack>

Index

Shipp, Ric, 71, 72, 73
Sickness Impact Profile, 75
Smith, Edwin, 18
spasticity, 61

T

tests, 63–68, 72
Tuesdays with Morrie, 97, 98

V

Vesalius, Andreas, 21, 22

W

Waldeyer, Wilhelm von, 24
Waller, Augustus, 35
Whiting, Marjorie, 56
World Federation of
  Neurology (WFN), 67,
  75

X

xaliproden, 74

Y

Yankee Stadium, 9, 13, 102